Toward a Science of Comparative Education

Toward a Science of Comparative Education

HAROLD J. NOAH

Teachers College, Columbia University

MAX A. ECKSTEIN

Queens College, City University of New York

The Macmillan Company
Collier-Macmillan Limited, London

To

Nicholas Hans

George Z. F. Bereday

and the memory of
Isaac Kandel

our masters in comparative education

Preface

When we met at Teachers College, Columbia University, while completing our work for the doctorate, we soon discovered that we shared common academic antecedents. We both had been undergraduates at the University of London, though on opposite sides of the Strand, and both of us had been graduate students in the Education Department of King's College, London, where Dr. Nicholas Hans introduced us to the systematic study of comparative education. Not only had we found the subject intriguing in its own right, but it had provided a natural focus for our common interests in foreign languages and cultures and in travel and study abroad. Each of us had spent some years teaching in London and had visited and worked in the United States at different times before deciding to study for advanced degrees.

Then, under the fescue of Professor George Bereday, our academic paths ceased to be parallel but separate, and we were jointly drawn into sustained and vigorous consideration of the methodological problems of comparative education. During that time, too, the periodic visits to Teachers College of the late Isaac Kandel, then Professor Emeritus, not only reminded us of the humanistic and historical strains of comparative education, but also symbolized for us the intellectual continuity of the field.

As we began to teach comparative education at our respective universities, however, we found ourselves united by yet another sentiment, a growing sense of dissatisfaction with the courses we were giving. It was all too easy to talk and write about experiences in foreign countries and to offer students colorful anecdotes and information about schools and peoples in different lands: this was, after all, the very stuff of our own experience and students so obviously enjoyed the telling of it. Moreover, even when this approach to the subject was rejected (as it had to be), comparative education, we felt, is more than the natural history or the comparative philosophy of foreign education. We came to realize that if its place in a university curriculum is to be justified, it has to promise some quite unique and characteristic assistance in explaining observed phenomena in education and society—assistance that no other subject can give better or as well.

For one year we discussed and planned a course of study to be given at Teachers College and then, first as a joint enterprise and later independently, we taught the course as a self-conscious attempt to develop in students an understanding of what the precedents of contemporary comparative education are and what the potential of the field might be. Relying upon the familiar empirical approach of the social sciences, we tried to grapple with some selected, substantial problems in education and society using cross-national data, and we attempted to teach our students a strategy and a set of devices that we hoped would enable them to make sense out of the mass of information and ideas comprising comparative education.

From this teaching experience we drew the present volume. Our purpose here is to describe, explain, and advocate the empirical method as a means of investigating problems in school and society and to demonstrate its peculiar appropriateness as a research strategy for comparative education in its present state. We begin, as befits those brought up in the humanistic tradition of learning, with the historical precedents. Part One is a critical review of some major contributions to the field during the last century and a half. However, we review them with a special purpose: to examine the authors' motives, data, methodological sophistication, and conclusions. Throughout the first section we seek to gauge the extent to which writers in the field developed a method of using cross-national data to make more valid statements about the relationships between education and society. We trace the progress from isolated, fragmentary, and impressionistic comments on foreign ways and peoples to the gradual emergence of empirically based social science analysis using cross-national data.

Two problems arise with such an approach to the literature. For one thing we were obliged to exclude much that is interesting about each of the authors selected. But even more important was the danger of reading into earlier writers much more than they themselves had put in. Clearly, the practitioners of the past knew only dimly the shape of the future of their field of study, and even if their knowledge had been better we dare not simply assume that they were interested in assisting in the formulation of an empirical approach. But we ran the risk of anachronistic analysis with our eyes open to it, hoping in the main to avoid it and certain that the risk is well worth running.

In Part Two we discuss scientific method as a tool of social science investigation in general and its relevance to comparative study in particular. All too briefly, we know, we examine that mode of thought called "science," the strengths of its explanatory power, the necessary primacy of hypothesis-formulation and testing, and the central ideas of quantification and control in research. We make no claim to originality here for we have based our discussions on some widely known contemporary work in the social sciences and we identify and explain a set of concepts that today are far from new. But we conclude the section with some consideration of the special nature and problems of comparative education as a field of inquiry and underline its urgent need for a firm and rigorous methodology based on the scientific model, hitherto lacking.

Part Three might be subtitled, "How to do it." It is the section generated most directly by the course assignments we have set and worked through with our students. It describes in detail each major step of an empirical investigation using cross-national data, from the initial formulation of a tentative problem to the critical evaluation of results. To make this portion of the book practical, as distinct from the theoretical approach in Part Two, we have used two model hypotheses throughout to illustrate the problems and alternatives facing an investigator at each step. In the conclusion we review the strengths and limitations of the scientific method in comparative education, and the appendixes contain some examples of alternative ways of handling the model hypotheses.

As we write this preface, we are for the second time teaching together the course we devised two years ago as a joint venture. More than ever, we are convinced of the timeliness and appropriateness of the methodology we are here advocating. Even during the short span of our collaboration we have witnessed an extraordinary growth of comparative work employing the empirical and quantitative approaches. We have been heartened, too, by the serious and mostly successful struggles of our students to apply in research papers the techniques we are urging. From our colleagues at Teachers College, Columbia University and Queens College, C.U.N.Y., there has been a response that was always interested but never uncritical. We trust therefore that there will be something of value in this volume for newcomers to the field and for more advanced students, as well as for those already qualified to teach and carry out research.

We are conscious that in an important sense we have sung a single tune in this book, the theme of empirical, quantitative research, and that the problems of education and society also encompass phenomena that are more amenable to treatment in other ways. Hence, we would not want the complete comparative educator to discard from his intellectual baggage the concerns and techniques of the humanist, the philosopher, and the artist. But we have felt that comparative education will benefit more from this single-minded plea for introducing scientific method than from a refinement and elaboration of other modes of treating cross-national data in education. In any case, it is our firm conviction that comparative education will find its most cogent justification and its most fruitful form if it develops along scientific, rather than along intuitive, lines. We hope that this book will help in some measure to speed that process and thus realize the great potential that undoubtedly resides in the comparative study of education and society.

Our companion book, *Scientific Investigations in Comparative Education*, demonstrates, we believe, that our vision of an empirically based comparative education is already on its way to realization. In it we have drawn from the contemporary social science literature a collection of articles exemplifying the approach advocated in this book. Instructors and students should find that the two books complement each other.

In dedicating this book to our mentors, we wish in no way to implicate them in its shortcomings and errors. These are peculiarly our own. But in this way, perhaps, we can make some acknowledgment of the inspiration and instruction they have given us. To many others, faculty and student colleagues alike, we owe much for their stimulation, learning, criticism, and above all, patience. Faculty colleagues who devoted considerable time and energy to reading and commenting on our manuscript were George Z. F. Bereday, Lambros Comitas, Lawrence A. Cremin, C. T. Hu, and Jonas F. Soltis. Our profit from their observations was great; the reader must judge whether we should have heeded their advice even more. Among the graduate students whose help was inestimable were Richard D. Noonan, who perpetrated the numbers in Part Three and the Appendixes, Richard D. Heyman, who expanded our interest in otherworldliness, and John Van de Graaff, who did not permit his status as a graduate student to blunt his perceptive criticisms.

We acknowledge with gratitude the assistance provided by Professor Lawrence A. Cremin and the Bailey K. Howard Research Fund at Teachers College, Columbia University, which made pos-‣ sible a summer's collaboration on the first draft of this book.

Finally, we would like to express our particular thanks to Mrs. Shana R. Conron, who dotted our *i*'s, crossed our *t*'s, and polished our prose; to Miss Marge F. Rappaport, who cheerfully decoded our drafts and typed them; to Mrs. Diana Kennedy, who devised the sign that kept the world from beating at our door while work was in progress; and to Lewis Carroll, whose *Alice* made sense when much else did not.

H. J. N.
M. A. E.

Contents

Tables

THE DEVELOPMENT
OF COMPARATIVE
EDUCATION

*"I don't think they play at all fairly," Alice began, in
rather a complaining tone, "and they all quarrel so dread-
fully one ca'n't hear oneself speak—and they don't seem
to have any rules in particular: at least, if there are,
nobody attends to them . . ."*

Part One

THE DEVELOPMENT
OF COMPARATIVE
PSYCHOLOGY

Introduction

The purpose of reviewing the development of comparative education is not simply to trace through materials that have been examined many times before,[1] but rather to search out in the predecessors of modern comparative education those elements of their thought pertinent to understanding their motives for undertaking comparative work, the types of data they used, the ways they handled the data, and their interpretations of them. The analysis

[1] For example, George Z. F. Bereday, *Comparative Method in Education*. New York: Holt, Rinehart and Winston, 1964, pp. 7–10; William W. Brickman, "A Historical Introduction to Comparative Education," *Comparative Education Review*, 3 (February 1960), 6–13. See also (by the same author) "Works of Historical Interest in Comparative Education," *ibid.*, 7 (February 1964), 324–326; and "Prehistory of Comparative Education to the End of the Eighteenth Century," *ibid.*, 10 (February 1966), 30–47; G. Hausmann, "A Century of Comparative Education, 1785–1885," *ibid.*, 11 (February 1967), 1–21; Franz Hilker, *Vergleichende Pädagogik*. Munich: Max Hueber Verlag, 1962, Part 1; Brian Holmes, *Problems in Education: A Comparative Approach*. London: Routledge and Kegan Paul, 1965, Chapter 1; Friedrich Schneider, *Vergleichende Erziehungswissenschaft: Geschichte, Forschung, Lehre*, Heidelberg: Quelle und Meyer, 1961; Stewart E. Fraser and William W. Brickman, *A History of International and Comparative Education: Nineteenth Century Documents*. Glenville, Ill.: Scott, Foresman and Company, 1968.

reveals the gradual, unsteady emergence of an empirically based, social scientific approach in comparative education, the history of which begins with simple narrative sometimes naive, but often astute, and ends, for the present, with the application of the sophisticated methods now being employed in the social sciences.

The development of comparative education has been marked by five identifiable stages, each characterized by a different motive for comparative study and each producing a different genre of work. The earliest stage, the period of travelers' tales, was prompted by simple curiosity. Second came a period of educational borrowing, when the desire to learn useful lessons from foreign practices was the major motivation. In the third stage, international educational cooperation was stressed in the interests of world harmony and mutual improvement among nations. Since the beginning of the twentieth century, two more stages have appeared, both concerned with seeking explanations for the wide variety of educational and social phenomena observed around the globe. The first of these attempted to identify the forces and factors shaping national educational systems. The second, and the latest, may be termed the stage of social science explanation, which uses the empirical, quantitative methods of economics, political science, and sociology to clarify relationships between education and society.

These stages are far from being discrete in time: each of these types of work in comparative education has persisted down to the present and may be observed in the contemporary literature, and rarely can any contributor to the field be confined within a single category. But the categorization suggested, loose though it is, provides a convenient, unforced framework within which to review the development of the field.

STAGE 1

The first and most primitive comparative education observations were the tales brought home by travelers to foreign parts. Such reports were essentially the work of amateurs who included in more general descriptions of institutions and practices abroad details of foreign ways of raising children. These *rapporteurs* tended to emphasize exotic information simply because it threw into sharp contrast the familiar practices and institutions of their homelands. Curiosity was the mainspring of their voyages, and local color the attraction of their descriptions. Only the rare observer could extract systematic conclusions with explanatory value from a mass of indiscriminately reported impressions. In the form of superior journalism, this style of work remains a prominent feature of writing on foreign countries today.

STAGE 2

From the beginning of the nineteenth century, coincident with the rise of national systems of education in Europe, journeys abroad were made by travelers with a specialized interest in educational matters. No longer motivated by general curiosity, they went the rounds of foreign countries to discover information useful for charting the course of education in their own countries. This group of precursors of modern comparative education were predominantly educational politicians, experts, and activists. Often they traveled not at their own expense, or following their private interest, but as emissaries, sometimes self-appointed, of their national governments. They concerned themselves with educational theory, methodology, finance, and organization. Teacher-training, instructional methods, and alternatives to traditionally accepted curricula were matters of major importance for them. Though their reports now focused sharply upon the schools, characteristics associated with travelers' tales persisted: many of the reports took the form of encyclopedic descriptions of foreign school systems, perhaps enlivened here and there with anecdotes, but rarely explanatory. Of necessity, objectivity and detachment were lacking, for these educational emissaries, committed as they were to the cause of education in their own countries, mostly saw and reported from abroad merely what they judged would advance their domestic enterprises.

STAGE 3

This was a period, too, when exchange of information about foreign countries and particularly about foreign education was considered desirable simply to break down the barriers of ignorance that divided nation from nation. Encyclopedic work was still the fashion, but it was argued that the very process of systematically amassing and publishing information on foreign countries would require extensive exchanges of scholars, students, and publications. The resulting network of international contacts would of itself help promote international understanding, as well as the improvement of social and, in particular, educational institutions around the world.

STAGE 4

Coincident with the rise of the social sciences towards the end of the nineteenth century there came a recognition of the importance of the dynamic relationships knitting education and society. Education was seen as the mirror of society; but society, in turn, was molded partly by the schools. Changes in one were revealed in the other. The concern now was to understand the interaction of education and society by analyzing the historical forces and contemporary factors that had shaped both. Moreover, exponents of this approach were interested in more than laying bare the nature of these relationships. They began to consider the possibility of using their conclusions to steer educational reform and so engineer the future shape of society.

In this phase of comparative education, studies of foreign schooling became to a considerable extent studies of national character and the institutions that help form it. They relied heavily on history and tended to strike a deterministic note. Problems of cause and effect preoccupied comparative educators, but inevitably their discussion quickly descended into a familiar circularity: national character determines education, and education determines national character. Where to break in to this perplexing circle was a question not easily answered.

STAGE 5

A significant strengthening of the explanatory powers of the social sciences took place after World War I. Many governments improved the quantity and quality of their statistical series, and statistical techniques became much more sophisticated. Partly in response to these new possibilities, the social sciences came to rely more and more upon quantitative methods; and the demands of researchers stimulated the production of yet more statistical material. This was particularly true in economics and sociology, and in later years this trend extended to political science and even to anthropology. Quantitative methods were adopted not only in the social sciences, per se, but also in some branches of education, particularly in psychology and psychometrics. In this manner, the humanistic origins of the social sciences, which accounted for their early philosophical and historical emphases, were gradually overlaid by new concerns and methods of an empirical and quantitative nature. Comparative education slowly followed the same path.

Since World War II these trends have accelerated and the empirical orientation of the social sciences has begun to reshape comparative education. Contemporary cross-national study in education is thus founded upon the twin bases of vastly increased bodies of data and improved techniques in social science research. Empirical, quantitative methods in comparative education are still beset with serious difficulties, but there can be little doubt that their potential contribution to the field is so great that they will have to be reckoned with.

Travelers' Tales

"If everybody minded their own business," the Duchess
said, in a hoarse growl, *"the world would go round a deal
faster than it does."*

From the earliest days, the motives drawing men to visit foreign
countries have been disparate, from simple curiosity to the demands
of commerce, diplomacy, and study abroad. In addition, there were
always those who had to live away from home to earn a living. It
was quite natural, too, that travelers with such experience of far off,
exotic places should from time to time commit to writing, for the
edification of their compatriots, some observations about the foreign
lands they knew.

Not all the reports were designed merely to satisfy the idle
curiosity of those who were unable to travel themselves. For instance, at the end of the seventeenth century Robert Molesworth
urged his English compatriots wherever possible to travel abroad
in order better to understand the problems and possibilities of their

own political system.[1] Certainly in Europe by 1600 there was definite awareness that comparative observations might have direct utilitarian and even explanatory value.

In the main, those who drew attention to foreign examples were opposing that style of historical and political thought that accepted domestic institutions as sacred and unquestionable, ordained forever by a combination of God and Reason. They were advocating that human institutions be examined in the light of the facts of the real world and not with chains of speculative thought and deductive reasoning. Even in those early days, the value of an empirical comparative approach to understanding was accepted. Indeed, many books were published instructing the traveler how to discipline his foreign observations so that he might derive the maximum value from his travel.[2]

Nevertheless, most travelers' reports on foreign education were subjective and unsystematic, the colorfulness of their descriptions alone redeeming their lack of objectivity. One commentator, in tracing the origins of comparative observations on education to the early writings of the Greeks and the Romans, cites Xenophon's comments on Persian laws and education: they "take care that from the first their citizens shall not be of such character as ever to desire anything improper or immoral. . . ."[3] Xenophon described the training of Persian youth for citizenship and leadership, compared the aims and structure of Persian and Greek education, and even commented on the relationship in the two countries between education and socio-occupational status.[4] Even in this early work the major

---

[1] [Robert Molesworth, viscount]. *An Account of Denmark as It Was in the Year 1692*, third edition. London: 1694. See especially the author's comments in the preface, in which he condemns the idle and wasteful "Grand Tours" of the average young Englishman, and commends "the Travelling . . . of Men, who set out so well stock'd with the Knowledge of their own Country, as to be able to compare it with others . . . ."

[2] Thus in 1598 Philip Jones published his *Certain Briefe and Speciall Instructions;* in 1601 Robert Johnson translated Botero's *The Traveller's Breuiat* and in 1605 Sir Robert Dallington published a *Method for Travell*. See W. H. Greenleaf, *Order, Empiricism and Politics. Two Traditions of English Political Thought, 1500–1700*. London: Oxford University Press, 1964, p. 172; and E. S. Bates, *Touring in 1600, A Study in the Development of Travel as a Means of Education*. Boston: Houghton Mifflin, 1912.

[3] William W. Brickman, "Ten Years of the Comparative Education Society," *Comparative Education Review*, 10 (February 1966), 4–15.

[4] William W. Brickman, "Prehistory of Comparative Education . . . ," p. 32.

defect of this kind of report is apparent: Xenophon apparently reported in the Persian system merely what existed in the rival city-state of Sparta, which he greatly admired and wished Athens to copy. As Brickman notes: "It would seem to be easier to hold Athenian ears with praise for the Persians than with proclaiming the superiority of Sparta."[5]

There is evidence, too, that Cicero, Tacitus, and even Julius Caesar paid some attention to the methods of child rearing practiced abroad. Cicero, who had studied in Greece and who admired the emphasis there on training in oratory, asserted that the Romans could do better than the Greeks in organizing education, if they put their minds to it. Tacitus discussed the educational practices of the Jews, the customs of the early Britons, and the characteristics of the Germans. He too compared the practice of oratory in several countries. Julius Caesar in his *De Bello Gallico* (Book VI) commented on the educational aims and procedures of the Druids and attempted some interpretations.

This type of activity was not confined to the Occident. In an Arabic work of 851 A.D., Sulaiman the Merchant wrote of his travels to China:

> Whether poor or rich, young or adult, *all* Chinese learn to trace the characters and to write. . . . When the cost of living increases, the government issues food from its reserves and sells it at less than the market price, so effectively that the high cost of living does not last long with them. . . . If a man is poor, he receives from the Treasury the cost for the remedy. . . . In each town there is a school and a school master for the instruction of the poor and their children. . . . These school masters are supported at the expense of the Treasury.[6]

Four hundred years later, Marco Polo, the great traveler and reporter on China, wrote:

> The natives in the city of Kinsay are men of peaceful character. . . . They know nothing of handling arms, and keep none in their houses. You hear of no feuds or noisy quarrels or dissensions of any kind among them. Both in their commercial dealings and in their manufactures they

5 *Ibid.*, p. 33.
6 Jean Sauvaget (trans.), *AHbar as-Sin Wa l-Hind, Relation de la Chine et de l'Inde, régigée en 851.* Paris: Société d'Edition "Les Belles Lettres," 1948, pp. 17–18. The authors are indebted to Professor C. T. Hu for providing this and the subsequent citations.

are thoroughly honest and truthful, and there is such a degree of good will and neighborly attachment among both men and women that you would take the people who live in the same street to be all one family. . . . Much of this is attributable to their education in the classics. . . .[7]

And still four hundred years later, Matteo Ricci, who died in China in 1610, praised the Chinese in the following terms:

Of all the pagan sects known to Europe, I know of no people who fell into fewer errors in the early ages of their antiquity than did the Chinese. . . . The books of rare wisdom of their ancient philosophers are still extant and are filled with most salutary advice on training men to be virtuous. In this particular respect, they seem to be quite the equals of our own most distinguished philosophers.[8]

Some Western commentators were less impressed with the virtues of Chinese society. S. Wells Williams, an American missionary writing in the mid-nineteenth century, had this to say about the Chinese:

They are vile and polluted in a shocking degree; their conversation is full of filthy expressions and their lives of impure acts. . . . More uneradicable than the sins of the flesh is the falsity of the Chinese, and its attendant sin of base ingratitude; their disregard of truth has perhaps done more to lower their character than any other fault . . . the alarming extent of the use of opium . . . the universal practice of lying and dishonest dealings; the unblushing lewdness of old and young; harsh cruelty toward prisoners . . . all form a full unchecked torrent of human depravity.[9]

China was not the only object of Western curiosity in the East. During the period when Japan tentatively opened a door or two to European, mainly Portuguese, traders and missionaries, many reports by travelers to those far-off islands existed in Europe. Thus Escalante, writing about Japan in 1544, reported:

They read and write in the same manner as do the Chinese; their language is similar to German. . . . Instruction of the young is en-

[7] Henry Yule and Henri Cordier, *The Book of ser Marco Polo*, third edition, London: Murray, 1921, I, pp. 412–414.

[8] Matthew Ricci. *China in the Sixteenth Century: The Journals of Matthew Ricci: 1583–1610* (translated by Louis J. Gallagher), New York: Random House, 1953, p. 93.

[9] S. Wells Williams. *The Middle Kingdom*. New York: Scribner's, 1907, p. 835.

trusted to learned tutors among the nobles, while the commoners send their children to Buddhist temples. . . .[10]

Not only did Europeans comment on Asian educational practices; Asians commented on Asia. I-tsing, who studied in India in the mid-seventh century, described the university at Nalanda:

. . . [it] can truly be said to be the greatest center of learning. Close to ten thousand scholars study under 1500 teachers who reside in six colleges. The buildings are magnificent, with more than 300 apartments and a very tall building that houses an enormous collection of books. Here, not only the scripture, life of Lord Buddha, Hindu philosophy, grammar, and Pali are taught; many study law, medicine, astronomy, logic and mathematics.[11]

It is difficult for us to judge at this distance of time the accuracy of many of these commentators, let alone the sophistication of their interpretations. But some travelers, we know, were scarcely naive tourists. For example, Alexis de Tocqueville's comments on American education in the early nineteenth century illustrated his central thesis that American society had not only proclaimed the virtues of popular democracy, but had also actually committed itself to democratic institutions.

It is not only the fortunes of men which are equal in America; even their requirements partake in some degree of the same uniformity. I do not believe that there is a country in the world where, in proportion to the population, there are so few uninstructed and at the same time so few learned individuals. Primary instruction is within the reach of everybody; superior instruction is scarcely to be obtained by any. This is not surprising; it is, in fact, the necessary consequence of what we have advanced above. Almost all the Americans are in easy circumstances, and can therefore obtain the first elements of human knowledge.

In America there are comparatively few who are rich enough to live

---

[10] E. W. Dahlgren, "A Contribution to the History of the Discovery of Japan," *Transactions and Proceedings of the Japan Society* (London), **XI** (1912–1913), 239–260.

[11] "Our knowledge of the day-to-day life of Nalanda depends chiefly on Hsuan Tsang, who shows us the monastery in the seventh century as full of intellectual activity. Under its aged and saintly abbot, Silabhadra, Nalanda did not confine itself to training novices for the Buddhist order, but also taught the Vedas, Hindu philosophy, logic, grammar, and medicine. It would seem that the student population was not confined to the Buddhist order, but that students of other faiths who succeeded in passing a strict oral examination were admitted." A. L. Basham, *The Wonder That Was India.* New York: Grove Press, 1954, pp. 164–165.

without a profession. Every profession requires an apprenticeship, which limits the time of instruction to the early years of life. At fifteen they enter upon their calling, and thus their education ends at the age when ours begins. Whatever is done afterward is with a view to some special and lucrative object; a science is taken up as a matter of business, and the only branch of it which is attended to is such as admits of an immediate practical application. In America most of the rich men were formerly poor; most of those who now enjoy leisure were absorbed in business during their youth; the consequence of which is, that when they might have had a taste for study they had no time for it, and when time is at their disposal they have no longer the inclination.[12]

However, such acute observations and sophisticated interpretations were quite rare in the reports of amateur travelers. Mostly, they were replete with ideological or cultural bias and were characterized by unsystematic reporting. Information on education, rarely provided in any case, was usually fragmentary, and value judgments, though freely expressed, were unsubstantiated. Yet this entire body of writing, unscientific though it was, must be counted as the first stage of comparative study.

[12] Alexis de Tocqueville, *Democracy in America*. London: Oxford University Press, 1946, pp. 46–47.

3

Educational Borrowing

. . . this time she found a little bottle on it . . . , and tied round the neck of the bottle was a paper label, with the words "DRINK ME" beautifully printed on it in large letters.

It was all very well to say "Drink me," but the wise little Alice was not going to do that in a hurry, "No, I'll look first," she said, "and see whether it's marked 'poison' or not" . . .

Motivations and Assumptions

When Peter the Great embarked on his program of modernizing Russia in the seventeenth century, he set a precedent that has been assiduously followed by later reformers. He sought abroad for models of what his country could become. His answer to the question, "What has made Britain and Holland great?" was the existence of systems of training that gave them superiority in industry, commerce, travel, and communications. As a result, Peter, inspired by the English example of a Naval Academy and the Dutch example of schools of navigation, imported British teachers to staff similar schools in Russia.

This precedent was continued in the efforts of those nineteenth-century travelers who sought to draw useful lesson from foreign educational examples. All through the century, American educators were visiting the major European countries; English commissions were inspecting European and American schools; Russian educators went to France, Switzerland, and Germany. Toward the close of the century, Japanese emissaries were sent to Germany, France, and England to bring back useful information for developing the Japanese school system. Even today this motivation for comparative study is still very much alive. Official United States visitors to the Soviet Union have examined the contribution of Soviet education to Russian development, and the Robbins committee, charged with recommending reforms of British higher education, made extensive foreign tours.

In the nineteenth century, as reformers maneuvered to establish state responsibility for the provision of schooling, the precursors of modern comparative education were drawn to study particularly Prussia and then France, as models of well-developed national systems. In Prussia laws requiring each locality to establish and maintain a school had been operating for nearly a century. In France the revolution and the Napoleonic regime had produced a system of secondary education to serve state purposes.

The prime example of work in comparative education motivated by a desire to gain useful lessons from abroad is the *Plan and Preliminary Views for a Work on Comparative Education* of Marc-Antoine Jullien (1775–1848).[1] Indeed it is customary to see the beginning of modern comparative education in the proposals Jullien made in his *Plan*. Jullien was not only a cosmopolitan at a time of intense nationalism, but also an exponent of French Enlightenment

---

[1] Stewart Fraser, *Jullien's Plan for Comparative Education, 1816–1817*. New York: Bureau of Publications, Teachers College, Columbia University, 1964.

views. A rationalist, an heir to the philosophy of Condorcet and the Encyclopedists, he subscribed to the view that one should look at facts in a structured way and that on this basis alone, proposals might be made to improve the condition of society. Jullien's intellectual interests were most varied, his literary output was vast, and he corresponded extensively with Jefferson, Alexander I, Napoleon, Fellenberg, Wilhelm von Humboldt, and Pestalozzi.

Frustrated by politics in France, he turned part of his energies to educational improvement. He was essentially a practical man, preferring to base all programs to improve education and society on detailed, systematic knowledge of what actually existed. He saw that the first task was to develop an instrument for collecting information on schools in some of France's neighboring countries. Jullien drafted an elaborate questionnaire for this purpose, and he hoped that the resulting comparisons would spur backward countries to develop their educational systems. Thus he sought to do more than merely collect objective data. He was ultimately concerned with problems of diffusing knowledge of education, particularly knowledge of educational innovation. Influenced as he was by the ideas of Rousseau and Pestalozzi, he wished to encourage a practical, child-centered educational methodology that emphasized, among other things, education of the senses and preparation for life in society, all with a strong humanitarian emphasis.

A decade and a half later, Jullien's countryman, Victor Cousin (1792–1867), investigated education in Prussia solely to learn how the French government should set about instituting a national system of primary education. Cousin was a professor of philosophy at the Sorbonne and later Minister of Education for France; he operated within the same intellectual climate as had Jullien, subscribing to similar Enlightenment ideas. His report on public instruction in Prussia resulted from his trip abroad at the direction of the French Ministry of Education in 1831, and it described Prussian educational administration, the responsibilities of parents and local communities in education, the training, appointment, and salaries of teachers, and the content of curricula.[2] The fundamental

[2] Victor Cousin, *Rapport sur l'état de l'instruction publique en Prusse*, in E. W. Knight, *Reports on European Education.* New York: McGraw-Hill, 1930.

law establishing the French system of primary education, the Guizot Law of 1833, was based on his report, which also enjoyed a wide readership in English translation and became influential in the United States. In one important aspect, Cousin's work represented a sharp departure from Jullien's. Cousin's concern was to use a foreign example as a guide and stimulus to the development of the French educational system, while more universalistic, internationalist hopes suffused Jullien's proposal. But most nineteenth century comparative studies were directed toward nationalist goals, and Cousin was undoubtedly more representative than Jullien of the tenor of comparative work in the last century.

American educators, too, were aware of the potential value of the schools for what is now termed nation-building, and for improving social conditions. They also hoped to find better teaching techniques and looked to Prussia, Switzerland, and Holland for model systems of teacher training and supervision. John Griscom (1774–1852) from New Jersey was one of the first to report on "a year in Europe."[3] In his preface, Griscom cited three reasons for studying European education and society. First, the United States was expanding her cultural and trade contacts with European countries and consequently ought to know more about Europe. Second, after a period of bitter hostility between the United States and England, greater intimacy might lead to mutual understanding and a desirable pacification of relationships. Finally, he submitted, there were lessons for America to learn from enterprising developments in European education. Twenty-five years later, Horace Mann (1796–1859) reported on his grand tour of selected European countries in the *Seventh Annual Report to the Board of Education of the State of Massachusetts*. He too prefaced his report with observations on the value of the study of foreign examples:

. . . if we are wise enough to learn from the experience of others, rather than await the infliction consequent upon our own errors, we may yet escape the magnitude and formidableness of those calamities under which some other communities are now suffering.

On the other hand, I do not hesitate to say, that there are many things abroad which we, at home, should do well to imitate; things, some of

---

[3] John Griscom, *A Year in Europe*, 2 vols. New York: 1823.

which are here, as yet, mere matters of speculation and theory, but which, there have long been in operation, and are now producing a harvest of rich and abundant blessings.[4]

Though the British during this period were much less prone to look abroad for models to emulate, there were some noteworthy exceptions. For example, Joseph Kay (1821–1878) traveled extensively in Europe to examine "the social condition and education of the people," and Matthew Arnold (1822–1888) reported on popular and higher education in France and Germany to the School Commissioners. Kay's motive was to collect foreign examples of improvement in the conditions of the poor. Europe, Kay observed, had much to teach England. The question he asked was, "What accounts for the enormous improvement, particularly in Germany and Switzerland, in the standard of life of the poor?" His answer ascribed these improvements to two important factors:

I think it will appear from the following pages, that the remarkable improvement which has been witnessed in the condition of a great part of the German and Swiss poor since 1800, has been the result of two causes; viz. (1) The admirable and long-continued education given to *all* the children; and, (2) The division of the land among the peasants.[5]

Matthew Arnold, who was a combination of school administrator, poet, literary critic, and political and social observer, was exceptionally active in his efforts to establish in England a national system of education, particularly secondary schools. His practical studies of the French and German systems, which included detailed historical and statistical material, were designed to make a particular case for the reform of education in England.[6] The purpose and value he saw in comparative study was "not to wrest it to the requirements of our inclinations or prejudices, but to try simply and seriously to find what it teaches us."

[4] Horace Mann, *Seventh Annual Report of the Board of Education; together with the Seventh Annual Report of the Secretary of the Board.* Boston: Dutton and Wentworth, 1844, pp. 20–21.
[5] Joseph Kay, *The Social Condition and Education of the People in England and Europe.* London: Longman, Brown, Green, and Longmans, 1850, vol. 1, pp. 7–8.
[6] See particularly his works: *A French Eton.* London: Macmillan and Co., 1864; *The Popular Education of France with Notices of That of Holland and Switzerland.* London: Longman, Green, Longman and Roberts, 1861; *Schools and Universities on the Continent.* London: Macmillan and Co., 1868.

Though Prussia was the admired model that attracted visitors from the rest of Europe and North America, even the Germans on occasion looked abroad for inspiration. Thus, in reference to the Bell-Lancaster system of schooling, Ludwig Natorp (1854–1924) asked if "there is something in it that deserves to be applied in our [i.e., in the German] elementary schools."[7]

Borrowing from abroad could be negative as well as positive; that is, lessons from foreign study might serve as cautionary tales. They could as well indicate dangers to be avoided as models to be emulated. For example, William T. Harris (1859–1909), who published voluminous reports about foreign systems of education during his period as United States Commissioner of Education, hoped that an understanding of foreign experience might serve to check the development of domestic peculiarities.[8]

Some observers traveling abroad to inspect educational institutions simply rejected the foreign models outright. Count Leo N. Tolstoy (1828–1910), writer, educator, and social critic, stands out among those in the nineteenth century who interested themselves in comparative education but were disenchanted with what they saw. He returned from Western Europe convinced that what he had observed in foreign education was completely unsuited to the further development of schools in Russia. Tolstoy was looking for an education that would set men free; he asserted on his return to Russia in 1862 that he had found abroad only what would make men slaves. Consequently, he rejected outright the desirability of Russia's borrowing from the West:

But what historical right have we Russians to say that our schools for the people should be like European schools, when we have none? Having studied the European history of education we are convinced that we Russians cannot build up teachers' seminaries on a German model, or transfer here German methods, the English Infant School, the French lycée, and special institutions, and in this way overtake Europe. . . . There is no eternal law of compulsion, common to all, which would justify compulsory school attendance against the wishes of the people. In consequence any imitation of European legislation on compulsory school attendance would be a step backwards and not forwards, would

[7] Quoted in Hausmann, *op. cit.*, p. 4.
[8] United States Commissioner of Education, *Annual Report, 1888–1889*, vol. 1. Washington, D.C.: Government Printing Office, 1891, p. xix.

be treason to our people. . . . If we are convinced that popular education has taken a wrong direction in Europe, then we should do better for our people's education by doing nothing, than by introducing by compulsion, all kinds of measures which various people consider good. . . .[9]

Especially noteworthy is Tolstoy's vehement rejection of the Prussian system as a model for his own country, at a time when admiration for Prussian schools was widespread among comparative observers, whether from representative or autocratic political systems.

One of the few American observers prepared to dismiss outright the possibility of improving education in the United States by imitating foreign examples was Francis Wayland (1796–1865), President of Brown University, who undertook a tour of England at mid-century. He condemned slavish imitation of the Oxford-Cambridge University tradition ". . . without considering how utterly unsuited to our condition must be institutions founded for the education of the medieval clergy, and modified by the pressure of an all-powerful aristocracy."[10]

At about the same time, the superintendent of common schools in Connecticut, Henry Barnard (1811–1900), though generally impressed by the superiority of European teacher training systems and schooling, voiced similar doubts. He asserted that Europe still did not manage to turn out "such practical and efficient men as our own common schools acting in concert with our religious, social, and political institutions."[11] If the aim in bringing up young people is not merely instruction, he argued, but the building of national character, the school is not everything. The quality of its output will be determined by a combination of influences derived from school, home, and society. Thus, though foreign institutions may be admired, they are not to be borrowed without careful thought.

Perhaps nothing illustrates the range of possible reactions to the impact of foreign example more vividly than the contrast between

[9] L. N. Tolstoy, "On Popular Education," *Yasnaia Poliana*, 1 (January 1861), quoted in Nicholas Hans, *The Russian Tradition in Education.* London: Routledge and Kegan Paul, 1963, pp. 92–93.
[10] Francis Wayland, *The Education Demanded by the People of the U. States.* Boston: Phillips, Sampson, 1855, p. 28.
[11] Henry Barnard, *Eighth Annual Report*, 1853, quoted in J. S. Brubacher (ed.), *Henry Barnard on Education.* New York: McGraw Hill, 1931, p. 75.

Chinese and Japanese attitudes to Western institutions and practices in the second half of the nineteenth century. Whereas Japan after the Tokugawas set out systematically to cull from abroad the best and most profitable lessons that the nations of the West had to teach, and even imported foreign advisors, the official Chinese establishment was loath to expose the country too widely and too rapidly to foreign "barbarian" ideas.[12]

Feasibility of Borrowing

It was one thing to assert that the study of foreign education was a valuable enterprise; it was quite another to believe that foreign examples could be imported and domesticated. Jullien, for instance, assumed that it was enough to establish the mechanism for collecting and publishing the facts about foreign education. It would then stand to reason that countries shown to be falling behind would and could adopt swiftly and without undue difficulty the examples of the leaders.

Victor Cousin's position on the question of the feasibility of international borrowing of institutions is instructive. His report on Prussian education was full of glowing praise for the primary and secondary schools, the institutions of teacher training, and for the benevolent despotism of the centralized administration; but he was also conscious that France could not just borrow what the Prussians had done without carefully considering the different histories, local government structures, and educational experiences of the two countries. He recognized the existence of "deep rivalries and sensitivities" between France and Prussia, which might impede the possibility of learning useful lessons from abroad, and he insisted that successful borrowing from Prussia was possible only given a

[12] Cf. Herbert Passin, *Society and Education in Japan.* New York: Bureau of Publications, Teachers College, Columbia University, 1965, chap. 3; and Y. C. Wang, *Chinese Intellectuals and the West.* Chapel Hill: University of North Carolina Press, 1966, chap. 1–3.

certain "condition préalable" (prior condition) in France. The ground had to be ready in terms of public expectations and willingness to adopt the institution or procedure to be borrowed.

However, whatever doubts Cousin might have had about the actual outcome of French attempts to borrow from Prussia were quickly dismissed on strictly nationalist grounds. He asserted that the strength of French culture and "the indestructible unity of our national character" would permit France to assimilate what was good from other countries, while remaining true to her own traditions:

> The true greatness of a people does not consist in imitating nothing from others, but in borrowing everywhere what is good, and in perfecting it while appropriating it for oneself . . . we can assimilate what there is good in other peoples without fear of ever ceasing to be ourselves. . . . France is essentially cosmopolitan; this is indeed the source of her great influence.[13]

Calvin Stowe (1802–1886), a contemporary of Cousin, concerned with the development of education in Ohio, in similar fashion dismissed the problems of transplanting educational practices. Before his departure for Europe in 1836 Stowe had taken a strong stand on the education of immigrants, advocating that they attend school together with the native-born. He was interested in the instruction of teachers and went to Europe with a commission from the State of Ohio to report on education abroad. He praised Prussian developments and believed they could be copied in the United States. Responding to critics who called the Prussian plan visionary and impractical, he wrote, "It can be done, for it has been done, it is done, and it ought to be done. If it can be done in Europe, I believe it can be done in the United States: if it can be done in Prussia, I know it can be done in Ohio."[14] Though he was aware that the new wave of education in several European countries was designed to develop loyalty towards regimes whose principles were

---

[13] Victor Cousin, *Rapport sur l'Etat de l'Instruction Publique dans Quelques Pays de l'Allemagne et Particulièrement en Prusse.* Paris: Levrault, 1833, p. 396. The authors are indebted to Dr. Walter Brewer for this translation and for other as yet unpublished information on Victor Cousin's career and work. See Walter Brewer, "Victor Cousin as a Comparative Educator," unpublished Ph.D. dissertation. Columbia University, 1968.

[14] Quoted in Knight, *op. cit.*, p. 307.

hardly acceptable in the United States, he was convinced that the State of Ohio could learn from European education.

Horace Mann, too, recognized that the gulf between the Prussian and American political and social ideals raised a problem of educational transplantation, but believed that limited borrowing was the goal. Replying to critics who doubted not only the wisdom but the practicality of a democratic America borrowing from a Prussia dedicated to monarchical authoritarianism, he asserted that the superior pedagogical techniques of the Prussian schoolmaster could be imported into the United States without "adopting his notions of passive obedience to government, or of blind adherence to the articles of a church."[15] Moreover, in arguing that useful lessons can be gleaned even from countries of antithetical philosophy, Mann implied that pedagogy may be regarded as potentially a neutral instrument, not inevitably tainted by the ends to which it has previously been turned. Different societies can employ common means to serve their own characteristic purposes:

. . . if Prussia can pervert the benign influences of education to the support of arbitrary power, we surely can employ them for the support and perpetuation of republican institutions. . . . If a moral power over the understandings and affections of the people may be turned to evil, may it not also be employed for good?[16]

A. D. Bache (1806–1867) was infinitely more cautious than Cousin, Stowe, and Mann about the possibilities of transplanting features of foreign educational systems. He went to Europe at the behest of the trustees of Girard College for Orphans and reported to them in 1839 on what he had found in visits to European schools, orphanages, and other institutions for the care of poor children. Bache's mandate was to secure accurate information that might help Girard College establish its procedures and methods. He was highly sensitive to the national circumstances in which educational systems developed and was aware that these local factors make borrowing extremely difficult. At the beginning of his report Bache observed that while the general principles of education might be

15 Mann, *op. cit.*, p. 22.
16 *Ibid.*, p. 23.

common to all nations, its general laws must be made applicable to different countries. He was one of the first to warn that:

Differences in political and social organization, in habits and manners, require corresponding changes to adapt a system of education to the nation; and, without such modifications, success in the institutions of one country is no guarantee for the same result in those of another.[17]

At best, Bache concluded, transplantation could be successful only if it were highly selective. It was indispensable to study the spirit, as well as the details of a school system, before borrowing. Therefore, he made comparative observations and evaluations, praising some aspects of one school or one system over another, but on specific points only—for example, achievement in the classics or a particular mode of instruction. He denied the possibility of using any single institution abroad as a model for the development of Girard College:

The plan to be presented to them [the trustees], as far as it is derived from these materials, must be made up of fragments, to be modified as to adapt them to the peculiarities of the College, and to our social and political institutions. . . . The trustees of the College have appealed to the experience of Europe to furnish data necessarily wanting in a new country, and it remains for them to apply the experimental deductions thus obtained from the old world with the vigour characteristic of the new.[18]

The running debate on the practical and theoretical problems involved in educational borrowing did not, however, seriously inhibit the nineteenth-century precursors of comparative education. From Jullien to Barnard and from Barnard to the present day, the assumption that there were practical lessons to be learned abroad has been readily made and acted upon. Indeed, many contemporary reports citing the superiority of foreign practices and proposing them as a guide to domestic improvement are lineal descendants of a phase of comparative education that began in earnest a century and a half ago.[19]

---

[17] A. D. Bache, *Education in Europe.* Report to the Trustees of the Girard College for Orphans. Philadelphia: Lydia R. Bailey, 1839, p. 3.

[18] *Ibid.*, pp. 605–606.

[19] Cf. Hyman G. Rickover, *Swiss Schools and Ours: Why Theirs Are Better.* Little, Brown and Company, 1962; Arthur H. Trace, *What Ivan Knows That Johnny Doesn't.* New York: Random House, 1962; Committee

Work of this kind in comparative education has thus extended over a long period, embraced many countries and educational institutions, and issued from the pens of an extraordinarily diverse set of authors. What these writers have had in common, however, was a conviction that something useful might be learned from abroad and a decided tendency to ride roughshod over the problems of transplanting educational institutions.

Data and Methods

Though influenced by common motivations and characterized by common features, the work of the early comparative educators differed in perception and scholarship. How far did these writers follow an explicit method and exercise discrimination in collecting, accepting, and interpreting data? The comparative works of Griscom, Mann, and Barnard all illustrate unsystematic approaches. Griscom's report was a conglomeration of jottings, one might almost say ramblings. Horace Mann went to Europe apparently guided by no system of inquiry, but prepared to report on whatever happened to catch his eye. In his discussion of housing conditions for poor and infant children in Germany, he not only expatiated on the "debilitating effect" of the German habit of sleeping between two feather beds, but for reasons best known to himself saw fit to append to this a lengthy footnote describing the ventilation system of the British Houses of Parliament.[20]

What was only amateurism in Griscom and characteristic enthusiasm in Mann became avowed purpose with Henry Barnard, who saw merit in the indiscriminate and even unsystematic recording and republication of *all* that was available. Barnard's contribution to comparative education took the form of republishing in English translation most of the educational literature of Northern Europe. The major vehicle for this enterprise was his *American Journal for*

---

on Higher Education, *Higher Education,* Appendix Five. London: HMSO, 1964.

[20] Horace Mann, *op. cit.,* pp. 50–53.

Education. For thirty years, issue after issue published commentaries by European and American educators on the administration, financing, curricula, and pedagogy of European schools. The avowed aim of this encyclopedic activity was to print

information which can be made available in organizing new, and improving existing systems of public instruction, and particularly institutions and agencies, designed for the education of teachers in every state of the Union. Its value does not consist in conveying the speculations and limited experience of the author, but the matured views and varied experience of wise statesmen, educators, and teachers, in perfecting the organization and administration of educational systems and institutions, through a succession of years, under the most diverse circumstances of government, society, and religion.[21]

The chief merit of all this material was that it appeared at a time when there was little available in America on the details of European schools, and what little there was had an extremely restricted circulation. As first United States Commissioner of Education, Barnard continued under federal auspices amassing data about foreign systems of education. His successor, William T. Harris, carried on this activity, though perhaps now somewhat more systematically, and Barnard's almost exclusive attention to European education was modified by Harris, who published information from more exotic countries, for example, Japan, the Philippines, Hawaii, Ecuador, and so forth.

The proposals of Jullien and the actual work of Bache on the other hand, demonstrated that even at a very early stage alternative approaches were possible. Jullien, though unable to realize any of his sophisticated comparative projects, insisted on the prime necessity of structured inquiry. His work in comparative education rested on four practical bases. The first was a proposal for an international commission on education with a permanent staff of international civil servants. The second was a questionnaire to be administered to a number of countries that would provide the information on which the international commission could make its recommendations. Third, there was to be a network of normal schools to train teachers in the most up-to-date methods. Finally, there would be a multi-

[21] Henry Barnard, *National Education in Europe.* New York: Charles B. Norton, 1854, p. 4.

lingual journal of education to disseminate information about innovations in education to all interested.[22]

The questionnaire was an ambitious attempt to collect facts in a highly structured manner. Jullien's *Plan* proposed an inquiry based on 146 questions, many with subsections, and even these covered only two of the six series of questionnaires that he suggested should be regularly administered. The information thus amassed was to be arranged to show trends and would be used to fill in so-called comparative tables of observations. Jullien was concerned in his original sketch with the twenty-two cantons of Switzerland and with some parts of Germany and Italy. He hoped that his method could be extended to embrace most of the states of Europe, with the intention of describing systems as they were, rather than as they ought to be. The questions covered all aspects of education, ranging from the specific, such as the age at which instruction was commonly begun, to a broad inquiry touching on how particular attitudes or emotions, such as courage, are fostered in young children. Although he was not primarily concerned with the effects of education on society, he did include questions about the effect of education on employment prospects.

Bache, twenty years later, also conducted his inquiries on the basis of a set of prepared topics and questions. He was required by the trustees to provide answers under sixteen headings on each establishment he visited: history, government, admission procedures, numbers of students, courses of studies, methods of instruction, systems of reward and punishment, "the general police" and discipline of the school, diet, clothing, and so on. The board wanted

---

[22] Apart from Jullien, only Thiersch stands out amoung the early comparative educators in his commitment to internationalist pan-European aspirations and to comparative pedagogy as a means of achieving them. ". . . behind the national coloring and the indigenous character (which education must have for it to be German and Bavarian for us, to be French in France, English in England) there is hidden a common spirit, *an embodiment of general principles, postulates, and forces common to all* with which, in the same way that the sap comes from the common root and spreads out in the individual branches, European man has broadened out the common trunk of his education." Friedrich Thiersch. *Über den gegenwärtigen Zustand des öffentlichen Unterrichts in den westlichen Staaten Deutschlands, in Holland, Frankreich, und Belgien.* Stuttgart, 1838, Vol. 2, p. 387, quoted in G. Hausmann, *op. cit.,* p. 11.

his examination to be "thorough and practical. They already possess, or may easily obtain, all that books can teach on the subject".[23]

Bache was an indefatigable observer, collector, and reporter. Using a case-study approach, he interviewed useful informants, studied appropriate documents, and then made his observations on the basis of a series of general questions that he adapted to the different situations. Yet even he thought it advisable to append to his report a list of the miscellaneous materials he had brought back with him relating to the organization of schools in Europe, and he included diet-charts, tables providing details of the time spent each day on different activities at various institutions, and remarks by eminent educators on assorted aspects of their methods. Bache optimistically justified the provision of this mass of primary material on the grounds that it might compensate for a certain lack of "vividness" from which the report might otherwise suffer.[24]

If the borrowing motivation for studying foreign education did not encourage selectivity in assembling and ordering data, neither did it encourage a due skepticism about its accuracy and representativeness. To take but two examples, both Jullien (who was explicit about the need for carefully structured inquiry), and Horace Mann (who was not), each in his own way failed to acknowledge the need to allow for error in the data he collected. Mann recognized that his observations on student-teacher relationships in Prussian schools might have been the result of chance or accident, but nevertheless he insisted on their validity. He spoke in glowing terms of the "beautiful relation, harmony and affection which subsisted between teacher and pupils." From this impression, he deduced that a community will obtain the quality of teachers it is willing to pay for. Teachers, he wrote, are likely to be "as good as public opinion has demanded; as good as the public sentiment has been disposed to appreciate; as good as public liberality has been ready to reward; as good as the preliminary measures taken to qualify them would authorize us to expect."[25]

Mann's conclusions, however, were supported by only the most fragile evidence. He had no guarantee that his sample of class-

---

[23] Bache, *op. cit.*, preface, p. vi.
[24] *Ibid.*, p. 3.
[25] Mann, *op. cit.*, p. 138.

rooms in Prussia was representative. Nor apparently did he ponder that an official observer coming all the way from America might expect to receive special treatment in the schools he visited, so that the evidence presented to him would almost certainly be biased. It is indeed extremely difficult to recognize the conventional school of Central Europe of the 1840's from the description Mann gave:

> I can only say that, during all the time mentioned, I never saw a blow struck, I never heard a sharp rebuke given, I never saw a child in tears, nor arraigned at the teacher's bar for any alleged misconduct.[26]

Even Jullien's incomparably more systematic approach to the data was no better calculated to avoid the dangers of unrepresentative or biased reporting. His prescriptions and preferences were everywhere embedded in the very tool he used to gather information about educational systems. He was a master of the loaded question. Question 124, a typical item, reads as follows:

> Has one tried to reduce the time given to the study of Latin and Greek, or even to retrench entirely that attainment of purely civic education, to replace it by studies better designed for the needs of each individual, according to the public, commercial, military, or other career for which he seems destined? In this case, what inconveniences, or what advantages have resulted from such an attempt?[27]

Throughout the questionnaire Jullien's assumptions about the proper goals of education colored the questions he asked.

Nor did Jullien recognize or confront the problems of cultural and ideological bias that inevitably would have arisen had responses to his questionnaire ever been gathered, either by international officials, as Jullien proposed, or by national civil servants. If international officials were to collect the information, they would run the risk of being too remote from the culture of the country on which they were to report. Hence, their answers might distort the actual picture by ignoring the peculiar national context in which the educational system operates. On the other hand, if national civil servants were to supply the answers, there might be real danger of distortion arising either from deliberate suppression of unfavorable information or from culturally biased responses.

---

[26] *Ibid.*, p. 137.
[27] Fraser, *op. cit.*, p. 80.

Most writers in this stage of comparative education ignored not only the rather obvious pitfalls of cultural bias, but also the technical problems arising from international differences in terminology and statistical procedures. Is a school the same thing everywhere? Are attendance figures collected on a uniform basis in different countries? Can it lightly be assumed that the cultural overtones of music education in Prussia held true for music education in the state of Massachusetts? These and similar questions were rarely raised.

Jullien, Bache, Arnold, and Harris were exceptions in this respect. Jullien hoped that comparative observations would eventually make possible a "positive science" of education. He saw a close analogy between "researches on comparative anatomy [that] have advanced the science of anatomy" and comparative education. He therefore hoped that the construction of his "comparative tables of observations" would provide a scale for measuring the relative values of different educational practices and institutions. Though this procedure inevitably must rely at first on individual and subjective judgments, it conceivably could lead to the development of empirically based measures for comparison.[28]

Bache raised a different but perhaps more profound problem involved in comparison. He asserted that as far as Prussia and England were concerned whole systems of education could not be compared. In the absence of any system of secondary education in Britain one could attempt comparison only of single institutions ("instances") in an attempt to appreciate the whole. He trenchantly observed:

> The variable nature of the circumstances bearing upon the secondary instruction of different countries, renders comparison, except in a general way, very difficult. . . . The school into which the pupil is to be introduced, preparatory to professional life, though called by the same name, is essentially different in different countries. An English university, in its objects and aims, and consequently in its organization, is very unlike the faculties of France, or a university of Germany, and the secondary schools, which serve as feeders to these institutions, must be modified accordingly.[29]

[28] *Ibid.*, pp. 40–41.
[29] Bache, *op. cit.*, p. 503.

Matthew Arnold condemned uncritical use of statistical material and lack of attention to the definitions of terms when comparing the educational performances of different nations. He pointed out that whereas on the Continent central authorities collected extremely precise and detailed statistics, in England this was nobody's business, and he voiced skepticism about reports from English observers purporting to show that English school attendance ratios were quite comparable to those on the Continent. Arnold went on to criticize the use of a term such as "scholar," which meant quite different things in different national contexts. In Germany, he observed, a scholar was someone who had gone through an extremely formal and prolonged period of academic training; in England any child in any so-called school was called a scholar. Moreover, in Germany, a scholar was taught by a teacher who had been trained and certified. In England no such uniformly high level of professionalism could be assumed. Arnold was almost alone in his condemnation of the use of like terms to describe quite different educational phenomena, and while he did not dismiss out of hand the use of statistical investigations in educational inquiry, he insisted that all statistical investigations be soundly based and comprehensive.[30]

In the reports on foreign education that Harris published as United States Commissioner, the already noticeable trend toward quantification became ever more pronounced. The reports were replete with tables of comparative statistics; refinements such as bar charts helped clarify the presentation. However, Harris warned the reader that the statistics were only approximately correct, and he referred to the many obstacles to collecting accurate data. Like Arnold, he noted the inaccuracy of local records and the difficulties of terminology. "We are not yet sure that the item which we call enrollment corresponds precisely to what the French and Germans express by the words *inscrit* and *eingeschrieben*."[31] Moreover, even with accurate and complete records and defined terms, there may be important differences in statistical procedures which make comparisons difficult. Thus,

[30] Paul Nash (ed.), *Culture and the State: Matthew Arnold and Continental Education.* New York: Teachers College Press, 1966, pp. 150–155.

[31] United States Commissioner of Education. *Annual Report, 1888-1889,* Vol. 1, Washington, D.C.: Government Printing Office, 1891, p. xix.

It seems, too, that they [French and German statisticians] do not find the item of average attendance by averaging the daily count. They take the attendance on two selected days of the year and make the average of these two days stand for the average attendance for the year. That this method can furnish only approximate results is evident. Both days selected might prove stormy or unusually pleasant; they would scarcely be average days.[32]

Moreover, with all his interest in collecting reliable comparative educational data of an objective kind, Harris insisted that these statistics took on meaning only in the context of national purposes and aims.[33] Any reports of recent developments in a given country, Harris asserted, must be preceded by an historical review of the earlier developments in that country that alone give meaning to the more recent events.[34] But while the reports issued under Harris's name certainly contained a wealth of background information, the reader was left to make his own connections between the historical narrative and the more recent developments.

Clearly, during this initial phase of work in comparative education the desire to learn useful lessons from abroad provided an indispensable stimulus to foreign travel and study. What it did not and perhaps could not provide was causal explanation. Given the motive—borrowing—all that could emerge at best were more or less sophisticated taxonomies. Unfortunately, and quite commonly, the motive distorted the perception of the observers, predetermined the types of data deemed relevant, and biased the interpretations they elicited from them. Whether the motive for borrowing from abroad was to strengthen the national state or ameliorate the condition of the poor (and both motivations were strongly represented among the comparative observers discussed), the borrowing approach led inevitably to serious methodological deficiencies. The a priori assumption was blithely made that institutions, even whole systems, could be reproduced at will on foreign soil, given only that their existence abroad was known, that sufficient information about them was available, and that somehow or other the ground at home was prepared for their reception. This assumption precluded what-

---

[32] *Ibid.*, pp. xix–xx.
[33] W. T. Harris, "Editor's preface" in Fabian Ware, *Educational Foundations of Trade and Industry*. New York: Appleton, 1901.
[34] United States Commissioner of Education, *op. cit.*, vol. 1, p. xxiv.

ever incentive there might have been to seek causal explanations of educational phenomena, to test the validity of a priori propositions, or even to give prime place to assessing the reliability, accuracy, and representativeness of data. It would be absurd to be overcritical of the failure of the early workers to carry out these three tasks, since they still represent the unfinished business of the field, but it is necessary to recognize the existence of substantial weaknesses in much of the work done under the aegis of the motive to borrow useful lessons from abroad.

4

International Cooperation

" 'Oh, 'tis love, 'tis love, that makes the world go round!' "
"Somebody said," Alice whispered, "that it's done by everybody minding their own business!"

If curiosity first prompted interest in foreign schools and the desire to learn useful lessons reinforced this interest, a further distinct and important attraction of comparative education was the hope that it would serve the wider interests of humanity, and not just the narrow purposes of national aggrandizement. Jullien was typically ahead of his time in calling for a set of international institutions to help tie the nations of Europe more closely together; it was not until the late nineteenth and early twentieth centuries that individuals who shared Jullien's hopes sponsored international organizations, conferences, and publications on educational topics. These international educators came from many countries: Herman Molkenboer, a Dutch lawyer, founded a trilingual journal to disseminate educational information, promote the establishment of an international council of education, and foster world peace; Edward Peeters distributed a quarterly bibliography of education books from Ostend, Belgium, and wrote a constitution for a proposed international bureau of education; Francis Kemeny, a Hungarian, proposed a comprehensive program of action in international education, to be subsidized from governmental and nongovernmental sources; and Fannie Fern Andrews, an American, enlisted the support of educational leaders in many countries for the idea of establishing an international bureau of education with special responsibilities for translating, publishing, and disseminating educational information—all with the aim of promoting world harmony. These and many other efforts failed to take firm shape until after World War I, and more than a century passed before a permanent organization of the type Jullien had envisaged came into being, in the form of the International Bureau of Education (I. B. E.), Geneva.[1]

Four types of work were characteristic of this motivation for undertaking comparative education. The first comprised studies of educational problems that appeared to be broadly international in scope. The twentieth-century comparative educators were strongly imbued with humanitarian and internationalist sentiments. They believed that those who studied education had an obligation to contribute to the solution of the world's gravest social and political problems, especially those arising from nationalism. The work of Paul Monroe (1869–1947) exemplifies this preoccupation. His essays in comparative education were published in two volumes (1927 and 1932) and collected his work in the field over the previous years. They include a series of studies of selected countries and essays discussing specific problems presented as part of social and political history. Monroe was concerned with nationalism, cultural revolution, industrialization, and the reconciliation of Eastern and Western cultural values. Writing after the devastation wrought by

[1] See Pedro Rosselló, *Forerunners of the International Bureau of Education.* London: Evans Brothers, [1944]; also David G. Scanlon (ed.), *International Education: A Documentary History.* New York: Bureau of Publications, Teachers College, Columbia University, 1960.

World War I and in a period of rising international tensions, he saw in the removal of ignorance a great promise for world peace and national stability.

Part of the unstable international situation of our present time is due to the fact that prejudice, misinformation, or ignorance of a politically powerful group of people may be an actual asset to their none too scrupulous leaders, and at the same time may constitute an international liability.[2]

These sentiments represent the extension into the twentieth century of an earlier humanitarian concern to use education for social amelioration. However, action was now raised from the level of simple bilateral borrowing to the plane of international discussion and decision. The work of Monroe's successors, notaby I. L. Kandel (1881–1965) and Nicholas Hans (1888–   ), is charged with similar internationalist concerns, as is the work of the contemporary international educators.

The second type of work characterized by this stage of comparative education is the outpouring of statistical compendia and other "objective" data on selected aspects of the school systems of the world. The I. B. E. produces its *International Yearbook of Education*, which summarizes in standard form information derived from questionnaires submitted to national ministries of education. In addition, the I. B. E. publishes a series of reports on selected topics incorporating information submitted by many countries and reviewed comparatively in introductory essays. Since the establishment of Unesco after World War II, the publication of internationally based statistics and the comparative review of specific problems by educational experts have vastly increased in quantity and scope. Commercial publishing and philanthropic organizations have also added to the flow of information on education around the world.[3]

The analogy of such activity with nineteenth-century encyclopedism is obvious at once, although the existence of permanent international machinery and the collaboration of governments and

[2] Paul Monroe, *Essays in Comparative Education.* New York: Bureau of Publications, Teachers College, Columbia University, 1932, vol. 2, p. 69.
[3] George Z. F. Bereday, *Comparative Method in Education,* chap. 12. New York: Holt, Rinehart and Winston, 1964 for specific information on the printed sources.

individuals the world over now insure the speedier accumulation of data, more up-to-date publication, and gradual improvement in the standardization of classifications and definitions. Nevertheless, many of the fundamental shortcomings of the earlier stage of encyclopedism remain, notably dependence on national government offices for the supply of both educational and social data. Derived as they are from official national sources, not only may the data be inherently incomparable because of international differences of classification, but there is the ever-present danger of willful misrepresentation to promote national propaganda interests. Moreover, even if the data produced on education were absolutely accurate and completely comparable, the unwillingness to probe deeply into areas where national sensitivity is high, such as the relationship of social class, race, political ideology, and religious affiliation to educational opportunities, often seriously weakens their significance. Internationally sponsored inquiries tend to avoid precisely those areas of education and society where systematic investigation is most needed.[4] Furthermore, when data-gathering is motivated mainly by the hope that the common activity will promote international harmony and the results improve international understanding, publications tend to emphasize description at the expense of explanation and avoid dealing with the most significant topics in education. The tomes in which results are published then sit gathering dust on the shelves of libraries around the world, unremarked and unconsulted.

This is not to say that information about enrollments, number of teachers, expenditures on schools, educational legislation, and so forth, all cast in some standardized form and regularly published, is not desirable. On the contrary, it is the raw material out of which comparative research may be fashioned. Pedro Roselló (1897–   ), coordinator of the I. B. E. and professor of comparative education at the University of Geneva, has devoted the major portion of his life to the management of such data collection. He sees comparative education as part of the total effort of the international organizations to build bridges between the nations of the world, and

---

[4] Notable exceptions may be found, for example, Charles D. Ammoun, *Study of Discrimination in Education*. New York: United Nations, 1957.

especially between East and West.[5] One important conclusion Rosselló derives from his long experience is that the political differences between nations notwithstanding, educational systems all over the world are tending to converge under the impact of common social and economic forces. He has used the data collected at the I. B. E. to trace the shape and direction of these world-wide movements, and it is this type of work that represents the third category of comparative education arising from the phase of international cooperation, and that is closely linked to some of the research to be described in Chapter 5.

The fast-growing field of international and development education represents the fourth type of work springing from the desire to promote harmony and cooperation between nations. Since the end of World War II, the obligation of the more developed nations to come to the assistance of the less developed has received explicit recognition in the programs of educational aid established by UNESCO, the Organization for Economic Cooperation and Development, and the Peace Corps, among others. In sentiment and assumptions these programs have much in common with the phase of educational borrowing, though it might be more accurate to stress the present special emphasis on lending by the countries with educational expertise, rather than borrowing by those countries without it. International provision of teams of educational experts, planners, administrators, and teachers has become one of the characteristic ways in which a well-off nation can show its practical concern for the plight of less fortunate peoples. Sometimes, as in the Peace Corps, or in the British Commonwealth Educational Cooperation programs, a nation chooses to undertake a specific national program of aid; in other instances, help is channeled through a recognized international agency. In either case, a large part of the aid effort can be ascribed to the desire to promote international good will and harmony and to the recognition that one of the best guarantees of peace lies in the better education of poor people.

---

[5] Rosselló's concern for breaking down ethnocentrism is revealed also in his techniques for teaching comparative education. He requires his students to describe the educational system of their own countries or cantons from the viewpoint of a foreigner. (Bereday, *op. cit.*, p. 210.)

One result has been a flood of publications reporting progress in educational development around the world, and examining in particular the specific contribution of international aid programs. Another frequent type of publication is somewhat more theoretical, and tries to establish general guide-lines for planners and administrators engaged in providing or utilizing international aid.[6] It is not easy to perceive in all this literature any clear demarcation lines between comparative, international, and development education, but much of it does supply information not otherwise available on educational development in many countries.

Multifarious activities that are hard to categorize neatly should also be noted. Through UNESCO and the International Textbook Institute in Braunschweig, Germany, direct attempts have been made to improve international understanding by eliminating bias in school textbooks, particularly in history books.[7] Collateral activities to promote international cooperation in education and cultural development have been widely sponsored by groups and individuals. There have been coupon schemes to overcome payment problems in purchasing foreign educational and cultural materials and there are guides to the evaluation of foreign educational credentials; other workers are now examining the possibility of establishing international equivalencies in secondary school graduation certificates. The list of such activities can be extended almost indefinitely.

[6] See, for example, *New Educational Media in Action: Case Studies for Planners—I.* Paris: UNESCO: International Institute for Educational Planning, 1967; Wilbur Schramm, et al., *The New Media: Memo to Educational Planners.* Paris: UNESCO: International Institute for Educational Planning, 1967; and the series on "Fundamentals of educational planning" published by the same institute.

[7] See Scanlon, *op. cit.,* pp. 21–24; and *Internationales Jahrbuch für Geschichtsunterricht,* Internationales Schulbuchinstitut, Braunschweig: Albert Limbach Verlag.

5

Forces and Factors

> *"No, no!" said the Queen. "Sentence first—verdict afterwards."*
>
> *"Stuff and nonsense!" said Alice loudly. "The idea of having the sentence first!"*

The publication in 1900 of a short essay by Michael Sadler (1861–1943) ushered in a new phase of comparative studies in education.[1] Although intimations of this approach may be discerned in the work of some earlier writers (notably Matthew Arnold in England, Wilhelm Dilthey in Germany, William T. Harris in the United States, and P. E. Levasseur in France), from this point on, new prospects for comparative education were revealed that were more comprehensive, more analytical, and that had greater explanatory potential.

---

[1] Michael Sadler, "How Far Can We Learn Anything of Practical Value from the Study of Foreign Systems of Education?," reprinted in *Comparative Education Review,* **7** (February 1964), 307–314.

This approach was more comprehensive because specific educational systems were regarded as the contemporary outcomes of an identifiable set of historical and social forces and factors. The schools of a particular country, it was argued, could be studied only as integral parts of the societies in which they had developed. Parts of a school system could not be wrenched out of their educational contexts, nor could entire school systems be examined in isolation from their total cultural environments. The first work done within this phase characteristically gave as much attention to historical and political developments outside the schools as to the narration of events within the school system itself. Later this heavy historical emphasis was gradually relieved by the growing attention to data drawn from economics and sociology.

Up to this point many writers in comparative education had been content to offer descriptive material on foreign school systems, implying that such facts in themselves had something valuable to say. The rapidly growing social sciences and new work in historical method tended to deny that facts outside a context of explanation could convey much. This critique was reflected increasingly in the twentieth-century work in comparative education, which now began to emphasize dynamic analysis and explanation instead of static institutional description. The concept of causation that began to grow and eventually to dominate the field was combined with optimism about the predictive value of causal analysis.

No longer were the horizons for comparative education limited to simple cross-national borrowing. Now the hope that knowledge gained in the social sciences would have instrumental value spread to comparative education: by understanding the forces and factors that molded education and society, men might be able to chart the course they were taking, and, if they did not like either direction or speed, conceivably they could hope to modify them. In the period between World Wars I and II it was therefore natural that the field should attract scholars who were not only steeped in the philosophical-historical foundations of education, but who also believed in man's capacity consciously to improve his social institutions.

Early expressions of each of these ideas and approaches may be discerned here and there in individual writings in the nineteenth century. Matthew Arnold, whose concern for accuracy and comparability of data has already been noted, recognized the close dependence of education on culture and insisted on the indivisibility of educational systems. Thus, when he discussed the value of studying foreign education, he wrote,

The study of continental education will show our educated and intelligent classes that many things which they wish for cannot be done as isolated operations, but must, if they are to be done at all, come in as parts of a regularly designed whole.[2]

In the same spirit, he considered that proposals for change in English education would be sound only if based on comprehensive comparative inquiry:

. . . it is expedient for the satisfactory resolution of these educational questions, which are at length beginning seriously to occupy us, both that we should attend to the experience of the Continent, and that we should know precisely what is it which this experience says.[3]

William T. Harris, like Arnold, recognized the necessity of discussing and examining the educational system of a country as an entity, and he accepted the thesis that education and society are intimately associated. In expressing his belief that comparative historical study can lead to the formulation of general propositions about the dynamics of education and society, he employed a thoroughly Hegelian dialectic. He pointed out that initially the development of schooling was generated by industrial and military aspirations. However, further development of a system of national education tends to produce an educated electorate, which in turn becomes a stimulus to further social change, specifically the breakdown of caste and the promotion of democracy. Thus schooling, which begins as response, ends as a powerful stimulus.[4]

A contemporary of Harris, Wilhelm Dilthey (1833–1911), professor of philosophy and pedagogy at the University of Berlin, also stressed the total and dynamic interaction of education and society. Though less sanguine than Harris that general laws of development could in fact be formulated, Dilthey argued that this could

---

[2] Paul Nash (ed.), *Culture and the State: Matthew Arnold and Continental Education*. New York: Teachers College Press, 1966, p. 164.
[3] *Ibid.*, p. 155.
[4] United States Commissioner of Education, *Annual Report, 1888–1889*, vol. 1, Washington: Government Printing Office, 1891, pp. xxiii–xxiv.

be done, if at all, through comparative, historical studies that traced the pedagogical characteristics of different countries to their national cultural origins. Hausmann paraphrases Dilthey as follows:

In the historical multiplicity and varying spheres of systems of education, one "cannot hope . . . to find laws (general principles)." The individual character of these systems of education is however "bound together in humanity's progressive development." Hence, it is possible "to ascertain the direction of this development through comparative observations. Consequently from this method a practical result can be achieved."[5]

Believing that education should serve the larger interests of society, Dilthey considered that the lessons derived from comparative study might serve as possible guides to bringing education and contemporary society more closely together.

P. E. Levasseur (1828–1911), a French statistician whose contribution to the development of comparative education foreshadowed much of the recent work in the field, emphasized the importance of both quantified data and analyses of cultural forces and factors transcending national borders as the twin bases for explaining educational variations. The report he presented to the International Institute of Statistics at its session in Vienna in 1891 is typical of his work.[6] It surveyed ten European nations in area studies, each of which contained a brief history of the educational system plus information on the administration, regulation, and financing of the schools. Reference was made to the sources of statistics on primary education in each country and the author provided tables that were, however, not strictly comparable from country to country, because they depended on the materials supplied by the several national governments. The second part of the study dealt with analysis of the data and problems of comparative methodology. Levasseur drew attention to the limitations of comparison based on statistics

[5] W. Dilthey, "Vergleichende Betrachtungen der pädagogischen technischen Systeme der verschiedenen Kulturkreise und -zeiten und Schlüsse in bezug auf das gegenwärtige deutsche Erziehungssystem aus dieser vergleichenden Geschichte," in *Gesammelte Schriften*. Stuttgart: B. G. Teubner, 1960, vol. 9, pp. 229–231, quoted in G. Hausmann, "A Century of Comparative Education, 1785–1885," *Comparative Education Review*, 11 (February 1967), 18.

[6] P. E. Levasseur, *La Statistique de l'enseignement primaire*. Rome: Imprimerie Nationale de J. Bertero, 1892.

collected in different ways by a number of different national organizations. While presenting "synoptic tables," he emphasized the difficulties due to the different meanings given to the same term in different countries.

Levasseur's comparative statistical tables enabled him to rank countries according to a number of educational criteria, and he compared his rankings at the end of the 1880's with those of an earlier study he had made in 1873. In all countries he saw that considerable advances had been made, but he noted that the rankings were largely unchanged over a period of almost two decades. " . . . it is certain that the Scandinavian states are at the head, that Germany and Switzerland follow closely; and that the Low Countries, France and Belgium come in third place."[7]

Levasseur's contribution is most dramatic in his systematic and explicit attempts to relate educational variations to cross-national forces and factors. He first examined the statistical evidence for a connection between the religious persuasion of a country and its provision of primary education. Both within and among countries he found a consistent relationship. Protestantism and Judaism were associated with high levels of school attendance, and Catholicism, Greek Orthodoxy, and Mohammedanism with far lower figures. However, he made it clear that religion was not the only influential factor. He went on to examine the relationship between race and climate on the one hand and the development of primary instruction on the other. With the sole exception of Russia, Levasseur found that all the countries of Europe north of the Alps exhibited a ratio of pupils to population of more than one to seven, as did those countries in the Americas situated the same distance from the Equator as Central European countries. He pointed out that the countries of Latin America, which may have been as well developed politically as those of more northern countries, showed extremely low educational ratios, a fact he attributed to the climate. However, Sweden and Finland, he argued, have triumphed over unfavorable geographic conditions, and he ascribed this to the decisive influence of the religious factor. In considering race as an explanatory variable, Levasseur found that the Teutonic peoples

[7] *Ibid.*, pp. 123–124.

generally appeared to be the most advanced in providing primary instruction and he suggested that the factor of race might also explain the relative superiority of the northeastern region over other areas of France in this respect.

He thought politics, too, exerted an influence on the education of nations. Holding race and religion constant, Levasseur found that the democratic countries exhibited a livelier interest in the provision of public education than did countries under absolute governments. Nonetheless, the political factor could be neutralized by other powerful forces, and Levasseur cited Sweden as an example of a country in which an absolute monarchy initiated the drive for public education under the influence of the religious factor. On the other hand, he gave the example of the subtropical American republics, where an array of factors, including climate, race, political instability, and social institutions, combined to inhibit educational development. Levasseur throughout recognized that no single factor acts independently of others. All the forces and factors he identified are dynamic both in their relation to educational development and in relation to each other.

The work of Sir Michael Sadler brought together the major separate strands of comparative education exemplified in the individual efforts of Arnold, Harris, Dilthey, and Levasseur, among others. From 1894 to 1895 Sadler was a member of the Bryce Commission on Secondary Education and for the next eight years Director of the Office of Special Inquiries and Reports at the Board of Education, London. In this capacity he made his major contributions to comparative education. The Special Reports issued under his guidance were strongly historical, empirical, and comparative. Although they contained many pieces that were reportorial and replete with detail, he by no means limited their scope to description. Sadler drew upon a wide range of authors in England and abroad to analyze trends in educational developments all over Europe, while in his own contributions he employed sociological as well as historical data to explain the interaction of education and society.

The clear intent was to influence the making of educational policy in England and Wales by referring to the lessons to be drawn from comparative and historical study. But they were a far cry from the naive use of data that had characterized most of his predecessors at home and abroad. Although Sadler was very conscious that his work in comparative education had important implications for educational reform in England, he firmly repudiated the idea of direct institutional borrowing from other countries.

The real value of the comparative study of institutions lies, not in the discovery of devices or appliances which can be transferred from one country to another (though the frequent possibility of such a transference should not be ignored), but in realising what is the spirit which has made a foreign institution great, and then in finding means to cultivate that spirit at home, if so be that it is needed to repair some weakness in the national life.[8]

From now on the mainstream of comparative education was to be distinguished by the comprehensive and dynamic view of schools in society that permeated Sadler's work. Sadler's major theoretical contribution to comparative education is the axiom that the schools of a society must be studied in the context of that society. "All good and true education is an expression of national life and character. It is rooted in the history of the nation and fitted to its needs."[9] Thus, the concept of national character was central to Sadler's analysis of educational data. Though this limited the applicability to other societies of lessons drawn on the basis of evidence from one society, Sadler nevertheless submitted that comparison can be used for asserting general principles. For example,

But on two points of fundamental importance Germany is teaching the world lessons which cannot be too often repeated. It is a blunder to specialize too early in life. And the only possible basis for a successful system of higher education . . . is to be found in an intellectually thorough, readily accessible and morally vigorous system of secondary education.[10]

Sadler denied the validity of comparisons made purely on the basis of educational statistics.

[8] Michael E. Sadler, "The Unrest in Secondary Education in Germany and Elsewhere," in Board of Education, *Special Reports on Educational Subjects,* vol. 9. London: H.M.S.O., 1902, p. 56.

[9] *Ibid.,* p. 162.

[10] Michael E. Sadler, "Recent Developments in Higher Commercial Education in Germany," (*Ibid.,* vol. 9, p. 525).

To throw educational expenditures into one indiscriminating total is like lumping, in one addition sum, plus and minus quantities without having any regard to the signs that really govern the value of several constituents. . . . To add up all that a particular nation spends on what it calls "education," and to assume that the aggregate represents expenditure on progressive influences, would be almost as misleading as to add up the outlay on torpedo-boat destroyers, on an Antarctic expedition, on North Sea fisheries, and on a racing yacht intended to compete for the America Cup, and then to represent the aggregate as having been spent on 'naval preparations.'[11]

Sadler's second reason for rejecting comparisons based on isolated quantitative data is that educational statistics for the most part refer merely to the school system. Yet the school in many countries is not the only, or even the major, educational institution.

School systems alone do not constitute national education. On the contrary, a country may have some effective ways of disciplining and bringing up its rising generation without having any elaborate school system at all.[12]

Sadler's awareness that schools are only a small part of the education of a nation led him to the conclusion that school problems,

though of course in some respects a special subject by themselves, are only seen in their true perspective when they are regarded as being in necessary and constant relation to other forms of social culture. The educational question is not a question by itself. It is part of the social question. And the social question is at bottom largely an ethical question.[13]

The famous essay of 1900, "How Far Can We Learn Anything of Practical Value from the Study of Foreign Systems of Education?"[14] summarized Sadler's views on the dynamic relationship of school and society and on the value of comparative education. The title of the essay alone is enough to reveal Sadler's instrumentalist hopes for comparative education, although it is worth reiterating that Sadler rejected the view that particular elements or methods in a foreign system of education were "detachable details." His instru-

[11] *Ibid.*, p. 21.
[12] *Loc. cit.*
[13] *Ibid.*, p. 23.
[14] See reprint in *Comparative Education Review*, **7** (February 1964), 307–314.

mentalism had wider goals in view. A sympathetic and scholarly study of "the working of foreign systems of education . . . will result in our being better fitted to study and understand our own." Thus, for Sadler comparative education was an analytical tool providing the explanation and understanding essential for successful innovation and reform in education.

For the first half of the twentieth century most of the work in comparative education followed the path marked out by Sir Michael Sadler. In a series of major studies a number of authors, each according to his own predilections, elaborated on various aspects of the Sadlerian approach. I. L. Kandel's classic work, *Comparative Education* (1933), traced the close connections between the schools of Europe and the political systems in which they were embedded; Friedrich Schneider (1947) and Nicholas Hans (1949) identified the broad cross-national historical and social forces that determine the varying shapes of national systems of education; A. D. C. Peterson (1952) and Robert Ulich (1961) sketched the historical progress of education as part of the developing fabric of European civilization; Vernon Mallinson (1957) elaborated on the theme of national character and its influence on education. All were concerned, as G. Z. F. Bereday observes, with ". . . the social causes behind the pedagogical scene . . . [and with] a speculative treatment of forces responsible for educational practices."[15] They all sought explanations for variations in educational phenomena by means of careful and accurate observations within and outside school systems. Their work was uniformly marked by liberal and humanitarian sentiments: they saw in education the first best hope for mankind and in comparative education the greatest potentialities for improving school and society.

Following the main thrust of the Sadlerian approach, a collection of articles on European and North American education, edited by Peter Sandiford, made "an attempt . . . to explain educational principles and tendencies in terms of social, economic, and political antecedents of each country under consideration." Each author described the historical development of one educational system, and within each country-study there was an attempt to treat a

[15] Bereday, *op. cit.*, p. 8.

common set of topics. Sandiford claimed that the countries were chosen for inclusion in order to provide examples of different types of educational control and national spirit, namely,

Germany as an example of centralization and absolute control, France as an instance of centralization under popular control, England as illustrating in her system the principles of individualism and initiative, the United States as embodying the hopes of a democracy . . .[16]

Sandiford viewed national education primarily as a reflection of "the theory of state and society held by a people" and from this axiom he derived such categories as "absolute control" and "popular control." But there are serious difficulties latent in this approach. Though there is prima facie justification for asserting that educational practices are functions of political philosophies, there is no justification for assuming that the particular categories used to represent types of educational and political systems will help provide valid explanations. Nowhere in the book is the possibility faced that a category such as "absolute control" may not be uniquely linked with particular types of educational outcomes. Unless such a connection is demonstrated, the explanatory power of the category vanishes. Moreover, the case study approach, which Sandiford adopted, involved him in a one country/one category schema. Generalization from these cases is thus impossible, an inevitable shortcoming when a priori categories are applied to single countries.

I. L. Kandel's contributions are outstanding examples of a continuous search to understand the relationship between education and the political and social problems confronting nations. In all his work, both as editor of the *Educational Yearbook*,[17] and as author of an imposing series of studies in comparative education, Kandel advocated the use of historical, social, and political data to explain the variety of educational outcomes. He was a politically liberal thinker who saw the progress of humanity measured by movement toward more enlightened, individualistic, and democratic school practices.

[16] Peter Sandiford (ed.), *Comparative Education: Studies of the Educational Systems of Six Modern Nations.* London: J. M. Dent and Sons, 1918, p. vi.
[17] *Educational Yearbook*, vols. 1–21, 1924–1944. New York: International Institute, Teachers College, Columbia University.

His classic textbook, *Comparative Education*,[18] appeared in 1933, at a time when economic depression, rising nationalism, the emergence of modern authoritarian ideologies, and the problems of the democracies preempted the attention of educators all over the world. A glance at the table of contents reveals the author's concern with basic historical-political problems—nationalism, national character, the state—and their relationship to education. He assembled various sets of educational data on six countries and dealt in turn with separate topics: the organization of national systems, educational administration, elementary education, preparation of elementary school teachers, and secondary education.

Kandel viewed comparative education as a comparison of "variant philosophies of education based not on theories but on the actual practices which prevail."[19] Broad social movements, political developments, and intellectual currents swept across national boundaries and each country reacted differently to these disturbances. He concluded that the new progressive philosophy of education, though widely accepted in theory and official statements, in practice was adopted to varying extents in different countries.

Older countries (England and France) with long established traditions of culture are less ready to sacrifice what is regarded as the essential basis of their national foundations; other countries (Germany) seek to adapt the new forms of social organization to the progressive development of selected traditions as a basis of national solidarity; others again (Italy and Russia) seek to combine activity methods with political indoctrination, thus permitting freedom within certain rigidly defined limits; finally, the United States building upon a tradition that tradition must not be binding, emphasizes change and progress.[20]

The degree to which a country adopted the new philosophy depended on its unique pattern of historical-cultural characteristics, which either inhibited or encouraged the implementation of new ideas. "As is the state, so is the school," Kandel seemed to say.

Kandel's approach to comparative study went far beyond static description. Following the direction suggested by Sadler, he viewed the study of foreign systems of education as a challenge to one's

[18] I. L. Kandel, *Comparative Education*. Boston: Houghton Mifflin, 1933.
[19] *Ibid.*, p. xx.
[20] *Ibid.*, pp. 867–868.

own philosophy and a means thereby of understanding more clearly the bases of one's own educational system. Consequently it was not in the mere possibility of cultural borrowing that Kandel saw the utility of comparative study.

The greater part of the world thus constitutes today a species of laboratory in which, so far as education is concerned, varied types of solution are being attempted for the same general range of problems. If it is claimed that education is a science or that scientific methods should be employed in its study, the educator cannot afford, any more than the chemist or physicist, to ignore procedures which are being tried out under conditions somewhat different from those in which he is working.[21]

Common, powerful social and other forces impinge upon the educational system of countries and create similar problems; cultures respond differently according to their peculiar characteristics and antecedents. For Kandel the practical value of comparative education lay in understanding this dynamic process.

The forces and factors (nationalism, political ideology, historical antecedents, and so on) that Kandel identified as explanatory variables were obviously significant *in toto*. But his approach provided no way of judging their importance relative to each other. Nor was there apparent any criterion for the inclusion of some factors in the analysis and the exclusion of others, except on the basis of "self-evident truth." What appeared in Kandel's work as persuasive conclusions are in fact important hypotheses remaining open for testing. Whereas many of his conclusions are supported by a wealth of both detailed knowledge and broad explanatory concepts, and though Kandel aimed all his work at explanation, the goal was never altogether satisfactorily achieved.

Kandel extended the Sadlerian approach far beyond the earlier studies, which concentrated on the amassing of data, statistical and other, without explicit recognition of the requirements of explanation. To comparative education Kandel contributed a theory of school and society and a theory of causation. He deserves the commonly awarded appellation of "Father of Comparative Education" for his stress on the need to collect accurate data, his emphasis on

[21] *Ibid.*, p. xx.

the cultural-historical context in which an educational system develops, and his insistence on the importance of explanation. Although he was an undoubted master of the first two, his successors were left to grapple with the unresolved problems of the third.

Nicholas Hans, too, brought to comparative study a theory of causation and a search for explanation. The subtitle of his major work, *Comparative Education: A Study of Educational Factors and Traditions*,[22] is the key to his approach. Hans identified specific factors that he claimed have affected educational outcomes in different countries and cultures. They are the forces shaping education and they parallel the *Triebkräfte* of Friedrich Schneider, whose work in Germany and Austria was contemporaneous with Hans'.[23]

Hans did more than merely synthesize the separate themes found in the work of Levasseur, Sadler, and Kandel. By concentrating on relatively few factors and by discussing them historically and *in extenso*, he singularly clarified the impact of environmental forces on educational outcomes. He distinguished between natural factors such as race, language, geographical location, climate, and natural resources and ideological factors such as the major European religious traditions and the secular forces of humanism, socialism, nationalism, and democracy.

He used these factors not only as basic explanatory variables, but also to identify the fundamental problems with which modern educational systems must contend. For example, the factor of race does not merely enable us to understand the particular ways education has developed in South Africa and in the United States, but race differences themselves pose grave practical as well as moral problems for educators in both these countries. Religion, similarly, is at once a basic causative factor in the development of school systems and an object of continuing educational attention and concern.

Precisely because of his conviction that countries have common educational and cultural antecedents and face common problems, Hans was able to find ample justification for comparative analysis.

---

[22] Nicholas Hans, *Comparative Education: A Study of Educational Factors and Traditions*. London: Routledge and Kegan Paul, 1949.
[23] Friedrich Schneider, *Triebkräfte der Pädagogik der Völker*. Salzburg: Otto Müller, 1947.

The analytical study of these factors from a historical perspective and the comparisons of attempted solution of resultant problems are the main purpose of Comparative Education.[24]

Furthermore, comparison is to be undertaken not only for purposes of analysis but also for very practical reasons.

It permits us not only to compare existing systems but to envisage reform best suited to new social and economic conditions. . . . Comparative Education quite resolutely looks into the future with a firm intent of reform. . . . Thus, our subject has a dynamic character with a utilitarian purpose.[25]

In common with Kandel and Ulich, Hans emphasized the continuity of historical traditions in education. He portrayed the palimpsest of education in Europe as the institutionalization of religious and secular ideologies in flux over the centuries. Consequently, he viewed the common school, for example, as a Puritan artifact and the selective secondary schools of France as a product both of Napoleonic nation-building and of the secularization of the former Jesuit élite traditions. Though Hans' writings are predominantly historical, he was far from being a historical determinist. He stressed the interaction between the forces and factors that shape a national style and the schools that consolidate it. This dynamic view rescued Hans from considering an educational system as the simple prisoner of its past, but left still unresolved the question of the relative importance of the various factors affecting education, including national style.

Hans did not rest his analysis entirely on historical data. His recognition of the importance of natural factors and his concern for the impact of current racial problems on education made for a more eclectic selection of material. Nor, indeed, did he rule out the possibility of comparisons in the future based on quantified data. But he did not believe that a statistical base was as yet developed well enough to support valid comparisons, and in particular he asserted, "Statistical comparisons of numbers of institutions and students, of hours devoted to each subject and of equipment

[24] Hans, *op. cit.*, p. 10.
[25] Nicholas Hans, "English Pioneers of Comparative Education," *British Journal of Educational Studies*, 1 (November 1952), 56.

are meaningless without their respective backgrounds."[26] However, in a later article reviewing the work of Pedro Rosselló Hans rejected outright all attempts to imitate in comparative education the mathematical methods characteristic of the natural sciences.

To attempt to reduce all the multifarious activities of mankind to statistical tables and thus to imitate the mathematical-laboratory methods of biological sciences is to misconceive the fundamental character of comparative education, which is mainly a humanistic study and not strictly and narrowly scientific.[27]

For Hans, two common denominators provided adequate bases for comparative observation and analysis: the "factors and traditions" that have influenced education and the common social functions (for example, political socialization, selection of elites) that schools are generally called upon to perform.[28]

In the work of Pedro Rosselló Hans had detected not only a premature attempt to found a comparative education on the use of statistical comparisons, but a fundamentally misconceived approach to the field. But Rosselló did not, in fact, try to base his comparative study on "mathematical-laboratory methods." What he sought to discover through his study of the basic data accumulated at the I. B. E. were the recent trends (*corrientes*) in education and society, which might enable him to predict the shape of the future.[29] Rosselló's analog for the comparative educator is the meteorologist, who studies recent trends in the atmosphere in order to predict tomorrow's weather and to warn the public of what it may expect. He claimed that comparative education has analogous instrumental value for educational planners and administrators.[30] It makes possible analysis of current pressures impinging on education and society and it informs policy-making for the future.

Whatever the differences between Rosselló's and Hans' ap-

26 Hans, *op. cit.*, *Comparative Education*, p. 8.
27 Nicholas Hans, review of Pedro Rosselló's *La Teoria de las Corrientes Educativas*, in *Comparative Education Review*, **5** (June 1961), 75.
28 Nicholas Hans, "Functionalism in Comparative Education," *International Review of Education*, **10** (1964) 94–97.
29 See, Pedro Rosselló, *Allons-nous vers une Ecole d'action, de raison, ou de passion?* Geneva, 1944.
30 See Pedro Rosselló, *L'Education Comparée au Service de la Planification*. Neuchâtel and Paris: Delachaux et Niestlé, 1959.

proaches, it is the basic similarity that is most striking. Both followed Sadler in drawing data from many aspects of education and society, seeking multifactor explanations of educational movements and concerning themselves above all with speculation about the social forces responsible for educational practices.

Robert Ulich's work[31] in comparative education has been more single-mindedly rooted in history. For Ulich, the study of education is the study of man's attempts to improve his condition in the face of continuous social, economic, and political changes that constantly threaten the status quo. In accordance with his principle that valid comparison demands a common element (*tertium comparationis*) in the objects to be compared, Ulich restricted his comparisons to countries with a set of common cultural antecedents.[32] In particular he viewed historical trends as extra- or supranational movements that set the general shape of education, and he considered the specific national culture as the screen through which they must pass. Historical forces thus become Ulich's *tertium comparationis,* and justify the undertaking of comparison. New nations recently emerged from colonial status can be taken into the comparison only to the extent that they encounter the educational and cultural traditions of the West.

Inevitably bound up with the forces and factors phase of comparative education is an especially strong concern with national character as an explanatory variable. Vernon Mallison's work[33] took its stand on this concept. Mallinson defined comparative education as a systematic examination of cultures and school systems, designed to uncover not only resemblances and differences, but their causes as well, and also the variations in attempted solutions to common problems. In this he was at one with Kandel and Hans, but he parted from them when he employed as his major source of explanation the idea of national character, that set of "dispositions to thought, feeling and behaviour peculiar to and wide-spread in

[31] Robert Ulich, *The Education of Nations: A Comparison in Historical Perspective.* Cambridge: Harvard University Press, 1961.

[32] Cf. A. D. C. Peterson, *A Hundred Years of Education.* New York: Collier Books, 1962, a study of educational patterns in western Europe and the United States, which offers a similar approach.

[33] Vernon Mallison, *An Introduction to the Study of Comparative Education.* London: Macmillan, 1957.

a certain people, and manifested with greater or less continuity in a succession of generations."[34]

Mallinson discussed the conventional topics of a textbook in comparative education: aims and specific practices in school adminis-tration, the training of teachers, and the organization of primary, secondary, and further education in several European countries. But his reliance on the factor of national character led him to make such statements as,

The marked characteristics of the Belgian are stolidity, good humor even in the face of repeated adversities, individualism, tenacity of pur-pose, and a quick temper to defend his own private rights and liberties allied to a shrewd realism and an eventual readiness to compromise.[35]

Subsequently he described the Belgians as possessing tendencies toward recrimination, insurrection, and lack of discipline. If one takes the national character approach, it is difficult to avoid such contradictions. As soon as the attempt is made to portray each and every dimension contained in a national character and to use the concept to explain minor peculiarities in the educational system and the society, serious doubts arise as to the utility of the concept in comparative study of education. Although Mallinson provided a detailed analysis of the determinants of national character and its constituents, he did not manage to solve the major problem in-volved in the use of the concept. If it is offered as a theoretical framework within which the variety of educational phenomena may be described and accounted for, the conclusion cannot be more than the empty one that education is a function of national character. And if, as one must necessarily assume, national charac-ter is partly the result of national education, problems of circular reasoning arise that jeopardize the value of the comparative exer-cise.[36]

This survey of the works of selected writers representing the forces and factors approach in comparative education has empha-

[34] Morris Ginsberg, *Sociology*. London: Oxford University Press, 1949, p. 76, quoted in Mallinson, *ibid.*, p. 14.

[35] Mallinson, *loc. cit.*

[36] See in particular, Annals of the American Academy of Political and Social Science, *National Character in the Perspective of the Social Sciences*, Don Martindale (ed.), vol. 370, March 1967.

sized that their fundamental concern was to explain variations in education from country to country. Although many of them recognized that their studies might possess instrumental value in reforming the schools and improving the quality of life all over the world, this was by no means their dominant concern. They were primarily intellectuals intent on explanation, rather than activists in the field of educational policy-making. They sought their explanations not in a piecemeal fashion, but through comprehensive analysis of the interaction of educational and social phenomena. If there was a certain degree of circularity in an argument that said, "society affects the schools; the schools affect society," it tended to be regarded as merely an inevitable part of the complexity of things. Recognition that mutual interaction existed was for them understanding enough, and speculation about the factors at work promised knowledge far beyond anything that their predecessors had achieved. Moreover, the very comprehensiveness of their view called for more than history or philosophy and implied that from now on the compleat comparative educator would need to be at home in more than one academic discipline.

6

Social Science Explanation

"No, no! The adventures first," said the Gryphon in an impatient tone: "explanations take such a dreadful time."

Implicit in the major writings that followed the routes charted by Michael Sadler is the next phase of comparative education, that of explanation based on the concepts and techniques of the social sciences. Since the end of World War I and especially since 1950, empirical work in the social sciences has burgeoned. The rise of quantitative empirical research has been based on the greater availability of numerical data, an improved technology for storing, manipulating, and retrieving data, and the widespread use of new statistical techniques. At the same time, social scientists have been formulating more sophisticated models that can be used in the investigation of society and its institutions, and many of these models provide the theoretical structures within which increasingly refined data can be employed.

The relevance of these social science developments to comparative education is obvious, and a growing number of works in comparative education today employ the techniques applied in political science, economics, and sociology. It is this work that comprises the most recent stage in the development of the field and the following survey of some representative empirically-based quantitative studies completes the review of the development of comparative education to the present.

Some of the fundamental elements of the empirical method that characterize advanced contemporary work in comparative education and distinguish it from the forces and factors approach are to be found here and there in nineteenth-century writings on education and society. Not only are there sporadic references to the possibility of constructing a science of education and society, and to the value of formulating and inductively testing hypotheses, but there are also allusions to the presence of identifiable and significant covariations between educational characteristics and social phenomena.

Among the many nineteenth-century optimists who believed in the possibility of achieving a general science of education, Jullien and Dilthey advocated systematic observation and comparison of facts. However, they lacked not only the data, but also the concepts with which to organize and interpret them. An example of an early investigator who, after surveying the field, proceeded systematically to test an important hypothesis in comparative education was Kay-Shuttleworth (1804–1877, born James Phillips Kay). Kay-Shuttleworth was trained in medicine but abandoned it for administrative positions in the Poor Law system and in pauper education. He took charge of elementary education in England in the 1840's and travelled widely in Europe to survey the condition of schools and society. As a comparative educator, he hypothesized that the extent to which elementary education was developed in Europe varied with the effects of the Reformation. He tried to test this proposition country by country, using quantitative data on the proportion of the population in each country enrolled in elementary schools, and concluded that with the exception of England Protestant countries were more advanced in their elementary provision than Catholic countries.[1]

[1] See, Lewis Spolton, "Kay-Shuttleworth—Quantitative Comparative Educator," *Comparative Education Review*, 12 (February 1968), 84–86.

At the root of the modern inductive approach lies the assumption that educational and social phenomena are not random and disconnected, but fall into identifiable and significant patterns. In the comparative analyses of Thomas Babington Macaulay, the historian (1800–1859), and Joseph Kay (1821–1878), the brother of Kay-Shuttleworth, are intimations of the methodology destined to become common in the twentieth century.

In 1847, in a speech on education to the House of Commons, Macaulay, who favored increased public support for education, compared the historical experience of Scotland and England:

A hundred and fifty years ago England was one of the best governed and most prosperous countries in the world: Scotland was perhaps the rudest and poorest country that could lay any claim to civilisation. . . . The parliament which sate at Edinburgh passed an act for the establishment of parochial schools. What followed? An improvement such as the world had never seen took place in the moral and intellectual character of the people.[2]

On the basis of the historical evidence, Macaulay identified education as the unique causative factor in the divergent social and economic progress of the two nations. He posed the hypothetical question, "Would the Scots now have been a happier and more enlightened people if they had been left during the last five generations to find instruction for themselves?" Macaulay asserted that he would answer his own question by applying Francis Bacon's inductive procedure.[3]

Thus, he said,

We have two nations closely connected, inhabiting the same island, sprung from the same blood, speaking the same language, governed by the same sovereign and the same legislature, holding essentially the same religious faith, having the same allies and the same enemies. Of these two nations one was, a hundred and fifty years ago, as respects opulence and civilisation, in the highest rank among European communities, the other in the lowest rank. The opulent and highly-civilised

[2] Thomas B. Macaulay, *Speeches on Politics and Literature*. London: J. M. Dent and Sons, 1936, p. 361.

[3] Elsewhere, in an essay on Francis Bacon, Macaulay showed only qualified enthusiasm for the inductive method. He warned that in many cases the lack of representative samples is responsible for quite misleading and patently absurd conclusions. Thomas B. Macaulay, *Critical and Historical Essays*, vol. II. London: J. M. Dent and Sons, 1937, pp. 383–384.

nation leaves the education of the people to free competition. In the poor and half barbarous nation the education of the people is undertaken by the state. The result is that the first are last and the last first. The common people of Scotland—it is vain to disguise the truth—have passed the common people of England. . . . State education, tried under every disadvantage, has produced an improvement to which it would be difficult to find a parallel in any age or country. Such an experiment as this would be regarded as conclusive in surgery or chemistry, and ought, I think, to be regarded as equally conclusive in politics.[4]

Another example of comparative analysis based on a simple inductive approach is in Joseph Kay's book, *The Social Condition and Education of the People in England and Europe*,[5] an eyewitness account of the life of the peasantry. He noted the systematic variations between the condition of the peasantry in general and the quality of the laws and institutions that governed the life of the people.

I do not hesitate, then, to affirm—and the proof of this affirmation I shall immediately show—that the moral, intellectual, and social condition of the peasants and operatives of those parts of Germany, Holland, Switzerland, and France, where the poor have been educated, where the land has been released from the feudal laws, and where the peasants have been enabled to acquire [land], is very much higher, happier, and more satisfactory than that of the peasants and operatives of England. . . .[6]

Kay insisted, too, that comparisons were best made between situations in which important cultural variables were held constant. In one instance he drew conclusions from variations among several Swiss cantons and in another instance from variations among conditions in selected provinces of German-speaking Europe.

Germany and Switzerland are peculiarly instructive and interesting countries to a traveller, who visits them in order to study the effects of different political and social institutions on the characters of nations. In each country, people of the same race have been exposed to the influence of institutions of the most varying character, and in each, as

[4] Thomas B. Macaulay, *Speeches on Politics and Literature*. London: J. M. Dent and Sons, 1936, pp. 362–363.
[5] Joseph Kay, *The Social Condition and Education of the People in England and Europe*. London: Longman, Brown, Green, and Longmans, 1850, vol. 1, pp. 7–8.
[6] *Ibid.*, vol. 1, p. 7.

I shall show hereafter, the different results, invariably and without exception, prove that the more liberal the institutions, the better will be the people; that the social condition of the people is generally the direct and immediate result of its institutions, and that it is capable of an amelioration, of which in England we can have no conception . . .[7]

And again,

Perhaps, of all countries, Switzerland offers the most instructive lesson to anyone desirous of investigating the comparative merits and effects of different systems of national education. Switzerland is divided into twenty-two cantons; each of which has an executive and representative assembly, for the special direction of its own internal affairs. Owing to the existence and power of these local executives . . . the educational systems of the different cantons differ from each other very materially in many respects. For this reason, and because the members of each canton are accustomed to observe and examine the peculiar merits of the different systems, the traveller is enabled to compare the various results, and to avail himself of the experience of educational authorities, whose opinions have been matured by great opportunities of observation.[8]

Kay's implicit argument was that in order to observe "the effects of different political and social institutions on the character of nations," it is necessary, at the very least, to control for the influence of race. His significant contribution was to advocate the use of careful sampling to control for this important intervening variable.

The contemporary movement from a mode of study rooted in the humanistic tradition toward sophisticated empirical work based on quantitative data and employing complex models of social theory and structure could not have been achieved without the closest attention to problems of methodology. Indeed, self-consciousness about methodology is the mark of modern comparative work.[9] In

---

[7] *Ibid.*, vol. 1, pp. 15–16.

[8] *Ibid.*, vol. 2, p. 346.

[9] For example, Philip Foster, "Comparative Methodology and the Study of African Education," *Comparative Education Review*, 4 (October 1960), 110–117; and Andreas M. Kazamias and Byron G. Massialas, *Tradition and Change in Education: A Comparative Study*. Englewood Cliffs, N.J.: Prentice-Hall, 1965, Chap. 1, where the authors offer the social science approach of S. F. Nadel, in particular, as a model for comparative educators (see Chap. 9.) Also, Brian Holmes, *Problems in Education: A Comparative Approach*. London: Routledge and Kegan Paul, 1965, Chaps. II–IV, (an extended discussion of the application of K. R. Popper's concept of "critical dualism" to the problem approach in comparative study). See George Z. F. Bereday,

an article in the first issue of the *Comparative Education Review,* George Z. F. Bereday recognizes the lack of agreement among practitioners of comparative education concerning the methods appropriate to their field and stresses the importance of methodology: "The discussion of methods of comparative education is perhaps the most urgent task which those who research and teach comparative education must face."[10] In fulfillment of this task Bereday's book, *Comparative Method in Education,* is the first in English[11] aimed at the central problem of method and techniques. The book opens with a lengthy discussion on method, but Bereday's subsequent comparative analyses of specific educational problems are also deliberately intended as illustrations of his approach.

Bereday distinguishes four steps in the total process of comparative study: description, interpretation, juxtaposition, and comparison.

First description, the systematic collection of pedagogical information in one country, then interpretation, the analysis in terms of social sciences, then juxtaposition, a simultaneous review of several systems to determine the framework in which to compare them, and finally comparison, first of select problems and then of the total relevance of education in several countries.[12]

Though the sequence of steps possesses its own internal logic and has value in the practical task of organizing research, there are some important questions touching on data and hypotheses that remain to be answered. If we consider Bereday's first step, description, the problem remains of knowing precisely which pedagogical data are pertinent and when enough have been collected. A parallel problem arises in the second step, interpretation, in which the historical, political, economic, and social contexts are to be related to the educational data. No clear guide is given to the questions of what data are relevant and how much is sufficient. Moreover, ac-

---

"Reflections on Comparative Methodology in Education, 1964–1966," *Comparative Education,* 3 (June 1967), 169–187, for a recent comprehensive review and bibliography of writing on methodology.

[10] G.Z.F.B., "Some Discussion of Methods in Comparative Education," *Comparative Education Review,* 1 (June 1957), 13.

[11] Cf. Franz Hilker, *Vergleichende Pädagogik: Eine Einführung in ihre Geschichte, Theorie und Praxis.* München: Max Hueber Verlag, 1962.

[12] Bereday, *Comparative Method, op. cit.,* pp. 27–28.

cording to Bereday's schema, it is not until these two steps have been completed for several countries that the findings may be juxtaposed, hypotheses formulated, and the road opened for the fourth step, simultaneous comparison.

But without an earlier consideration of the hypothesis to be tested by simultaneous comparison, basic practical criteria for conducting the study are lacking. Without a hypothesis there is no way to decide which data are relevant in the early stages of the investigation, when data gathering may cease, and which countries ought to be included in the sample. Without a hypothesis, an inquiry can become exceptionally wasteful of time and energy. Relegation of hypothesis-formulation to the late point it occupies in Bereday's schema permits contemporary workers in comparative education to perpetuate the two prime weaknesses of their nineteenth-century predecessors: the indiscriminate amassing of pedagogical and social information and the dominance of a priori assumptions over both the collection of facts and the conclusions drawn from them. Indeed, in his article in the first issue of the *Comparative Education Review*, Bereday recognizes this danger quite clearly:

. . . no method is comparative unless it is preceded by a formulation of an abstract scheme which serves as a guiding hypothesis for the collection and presentation of comparative data. A pure enunciation of facts about foreign countries is in the light of this analysis not a comparative treatment.[13]

According to Bereday, attempts at wide-ranging comparisons can be ventured only after an arduous and lengthy professional preparation. The aspiring student must be prepared virtually to retrace the historical stages of development of comparative education, learning first how to amass data, then how to sort it, then how to fit it into its indigenous social and historical context, and then how to juxtapose these sets of information in order to produce hypotheses for testing. Only after practice in these tasks can the student successfully approach the apogee of his career, total analysis, which is a complete and concurrent comparison not only of many countries,

13 G.Z.F.B., "Some Discussions . . . ," p. 15.

but also of the many problems and facets of different educational systems and societies. But there are practical difficulties to Bereday's recommendations. Not only do few modern sciences require their initiates to recapitulate the history of their fields (*ars longa, vita brevis*), but it is questionable whether the very goal of simultaneous comparison as defined by Bereday is the right or practical one to set before comparative education. The need at this point is more to establish what contribution the social sciences can make to developing comparative education than to call for the creation of superscholars capable of simultaneous comparison.

Like Sadler, Bereday is a bridge between two phases of comparative education. Sadler connected the earlier data-collecting enterprise of an encyclopedic and somewhat indiscriminate order with the later works of such men as Hans and Kandel, whose approach stressed explanation rather than description and who sought that explanation in a study of the historical context and the influence of cultural forces. Bereday connects the historical-philosophical phase with two new emphases: a basic concern with the concepts and data of the social sciences, especially sociology and political science, and an awareness and explicitness about matters methodological.

Among the many problems of education and society awaiting investigation during the postwar period, two are outstanding. The first is the concern of economists: the relationship between education and the production and use of wealth. The second is the concern of sociologists and political scientists: the relation between education and various aspects of social and political change.

One of the legacies of World War II in Europe has been the development of profound interest in analyzing the sources of economic growth and in devising policies to promote it. Investment in education clearly plays a significant, though as yet largely unspecified, role. Within the European community, the Organisation for Economic Cooperation and Development (OECD) is a major international source of technique and information to assist planners in achieving the economic and educational objectives of their countries. In fulfilling this function, OECD has published a mass of relatively highly structured and standardized information about national educational systems and labor forces and the relationship between them.[14]

Although this work does not attempt to state or test any hypotheses about relationships between education and the economy, OECD has produced numerous statements and reports designed to be of practical value to planners and written at various levels of abstraction. They range from "bread-and-butter" publications dealing with organizational and statistical problems in planning[15] to highly sophisticated planning models that attempt to express mathematically the variety of educational-economic relationships within a number of countries. The assumption underlying this work is that consistent relationships between education and the economy can be expressed in quantitative terms and that the results generated can form the basis for national planners to predict and control change in their educational systems. Yet it is immediately obvious that mathematical forays attempting to link educational and economic development are rendered exceptionally hazardous by both the poor state of the data and the horrendous complexity of the socioeducational process.[16]

In a classic work published in 1958, Friedrich Edding analyzes educational expenditures in relation to national income in a score of countries and shows the presence of a very close correlation between the size of a country's national income and the percentage of that national income devoted to education.[17] Not only do the richer countries spend more on education because they can afford to but high levels of educational expenditure appear to be a precondition for further economic growth. Indeed, Edding concludes

[14] For example, The Mediterranean Regional Project, Organisation for Economic Cooperation and Development, *Country Reports*. Paris: OECD, 1965, 1966.

[15] Study Group in the Economics of Education. *Organisational Problems in Planning Educational Development*. Paris: OECD, 1966, and *Methods and Statistical Needs for Educational Planning*. Paris: OECD, 1967.

[16] For examples of mathematical models, see Jan Tinbergen, et al., *Econometric Models of Education: Some Applications*. Paris: OECD, 1965. For pungent criticism of this genre of work, see "Comments" by Thomas Balogh, in Study Group in the Economics of Education, *The Residual Factor and Economic Growth*. Paris: OECD, 1964, pp. 180–187.

[17] F. Edding, *Internationale Tendenzen in der Entwicklung der Ausgaben für Schulen und Hochschulen*. Kiel: Institut für Weltwirtschaft an der Universität Kiel, 1958.

that societies are by no means as free to determine the level of their expenditure on education as might be imagined; in an important sense it is determined for them by the level of economic development they have already reached.

Both in this and other work, Edding is primarily interested in the accumulation of quantified data. Because his main purpose is to examine the data in order to generate problems, he relegates the formulation and testing of hypotheses to a rather minor place in his work. As he says,

> It seems worthwhile to study in a descriptive way, the factors influencing educational expenditure and its relation to national aggregates in a number of countries. It seems useful also to analyse the proportions of expenditure by level of school and of government in different countries and in different phases of economic development.[18]

Edding's early empirical work demanded a certain degree of intellectual courage, even rashness. He plunged in and used data that were often far from perfect: not merely were they incomplete, but there were serious problems of comparability. This he fully understood, but he asserted that it would be wrong to abandon attempts to achieve comparisons while awaiting perfect data, for only by trial and error will matters be improved.

> There are possibilities of standardization of definitions and of enlarging the number of institutions reporting outlays on education. Each new survey has shown improvements, and even in the present state of statistics it is possible to learn much from expenditure accounts and comparisons of expenditure.[19]

Another attempt, but on a much larger scale than Edding's, to investigate educational and economic interconnections is that of Frederick Harbison and Charles A. Myers.[20] Two of their principal objectives are to rank a large group of countries (seventy-five) on the basis of a number of indicators of human resource develop-

[18] F. Edding, "Expenditure on Education: Statistics and Comments," in E. A. G. Robinson and J. E. Vaizey (eds.), *The Economics of Education.* London: Macmillan, 1966, pp. 24–25.

[19] *Ibid.*, p. 25.

[20] Frederick Harbison and Charles A. Myers, *Education, Manpower and Economic Growth: Strategies of human resource development.* New York: McGraw-Hill, 1964, especially Chapter 3, "Quantitative Indicators of Human Resource Development."

ment and "to determine whether there are significant statistical relationships among various human resource indicators and measures of economic development."[21] Harbison and Myers do, in fact, conclude that a number of significant statistical relationships between economic and educational variables emerge from their analysis. Their findings tend to support those of Edding in suggesting that levels of educational expenditure and development are closely correlated. More specifically, they show that secondary and higher education enrollment ratios are closely correlated with levels of gross national product per capita. (That the relationship between education and the economy is not always a simple or obvious one is shown by another of their findings: the very weak correlation between the percentages of students enrolled in scientific and technical faculties in higher education and levels of gross national product.)

The authors are at pains to emphasize that the close correlations between variables by no means signify causal relationships one way or another. "The data do not permit a conclusion that an increase of X per cent in second-level or higher education will *result* in a Y per cent increase in GNP per capita."[22] Like Edding, Harbison and Myers are involved essentially in a search for patterns of relationships between educational and economic variables. They concentrate a great deal of attention on the selection of appropriate indicators for the variables, and of necessity an important part of their work is to show that the indicators they do use are, in fact, valid ones.[23] A consequence of this concentration on the problems of variables rather than on the formulation and testing of hypotheses is that the authors' ability to provide causal explanations for the observed relationships is, as they concede, limited.

Mary Jean Bowman and C. Arnold Anderson investigate the role of education in development by posing the problem in more spe-

[21] *Ibid.*, p. 23.

[22] *Ibid.*, p. 44.

[23] Cf. John Vaizey, "Comparative Notes on Economic Growth and Social Change in Education," *Comparative Education Review,* 5 (June 1961), 7–12; and John Vaizey, "Education and Investment in Comparative Education," *Ibid.* (October 1961), 97–104.

cific terms.[24] They ask "to what extent is literacy . . . an essential ingredient of economic advance? To what extent, on the other hand, may literacy be superfluous or inoperative in early stages of development?"[25] By correlating levels of literacy with gross national product per capita in more than twenty countries, they find that there appears to be an economic plateau, where increase in income is negligible as literacy rates range between 30 and 70 per cent. On either side of this plateau literacy rates seem to be moderately good predictors of levels of gross national product per capita. The authors also correlate gross national product and enrollment ratios in primary and post-primary education in order to find connections between specific levels of school provision and the economy. Their conclusion is that

> The data suggest . . ., though they cannot prove, the occurrence of important, distinct stages in educational lead and lag; an early stage of education-economic breakthrough; a plateau in which diffusing education is still not sufficient to support a high-level economy; and a third stage in which another economic breakthrough is possible, built on a well-educated population.[26]

That the relationship between levels of education and the economic transformation of society is not a simple one is demonstrated by the fact that income levels for 1938 are far better predictors of income levels in 1955 than are educational levels for 1938. Bowman and Anderson, therefore, see educational investment as one factor operating with differing efficiency in different matrices of other social factors, but they do not attempt to investigate the interactions of these factors.

Alexander Peaslee discusses the relationship between primary school enrollments and economic growth and employs a similar approach.[27] He explores the hypothesis that the level of primary school enrollment and subsequent levels of economic development

[24] Mary Jean Bowman and C. Arnold Anderson, "Concerning the Role of Education in Development" in Clifford Geertz (ed.), *Old Societies and New States*. New York: The Free Press, 1963, pp. 247–279.

[25] *Ibid.*, p. 250.

[26] *Ibid.*, p. 266.

[27] Alexander L. Peaslee, "Primary School Enrollments and Economic Growth," *Comparative Education Review*, 11 (Feb. 1967), 57–67.

are positively correlated. This study is an example of a modest attempt to test relationships to establish what might be termed "middle-range theory" in comparative study, that is, to refine and make more precise the general proposition that school enrollment and economic growth are related. With only minor and explicable exceptions, Peaslee shows that the twenty-seven countries leading the world in per capita output by 1958 were the same countries that in 1920 enrolled 10 per cent or more of their populations in primary schools. The author goes on to use this 10 per cent rule to explain retroactively the poor economic performance of selected countries (India, the United Arab Republic, and Pakistan), claiming that their poor rates of economic growth could have been predicted from their undue emphasis on secondary education while the primary enrollment ratio remained below the critical 10 per cent level.[28]

M. C. Kaser examines the industrialized market economies to discover "whether any educational structure is common to the experience of those countries at corresponding economic graduations."[29] He hypothesizes that patterns of education development exist, defined in terms of the quantity *and quality* of formal education provided.[30] To test this hypothesis Kaser selects a range of countries that gives "adequate geographical spread, diversity of natural resource endowments, and variations in educational

[28] Cf. William S. Bennett, Jr., "Educational Change and Economic Development," *Sociology of Education*, **40** (Spring 1967), 101-114, in which the author focuses on the quantitative relationship between *secondary* enrollments and economic development. He remarks that the work "does *not* impute a causal role to either economic or educational variables. It assumes, rather, that these variables are interrelated in a complex manner. It will develop a set of universal propositions regarding these relationships. . . ." (pp. 103–104).

[29] M. C. Kaser, "Education and Economic Progress: Experience in Industrialized Market Economies," in Robinson and Vaizey, *The Economics of Education*, pp. 89–173.

[30] Cf. C. E. Beeby, *The Quality of Education in Developing Countries*, Cambridge, Mass.: Harvard University Press, 1966, in which the author also presents a "theory of developmental stages" of primary school systems. However, his categories are derived from personal experience, and although he asserts that countries must traverse the stages in a set sequence, he nowhere attempts inductive proof of this contention. He admits that: "Proof in any strict sense [of a hypothesis that such stages exist] may have to wait until the stages and sub-stages can be expressed quantitatively . . ." (p. 88).

policy."[31] The countries are also selected to represent different levels of income at the onset of industrialization. Kaser uses as quantitative indicators of patterns of educational development the ratios of secondary/primary enrollment and university/primary enrollment. He finds that "no pattern of education at given incomes emerges until the $650 to $750 levels."[32] Weak patterns appear thereafter and all through the higher income levels there are some weak consistent relations. Generally, however, he finds little support for the hypothesis that the industrialized nations passed through similar stages of *quantitative* educational development. He explains this by reference to the different pedagogical and social expectations prevailing within countries at different times.

Kaser proceeds from his examinations of quantitative patterns to investigate whether any *qualitative* patterns can be detected. One important measure of school quality does indeed appear to change systematically as GNP per capita rises: the higher the GNP per capita, the smaller the student-teacher ratio. However, there is no systematic variation in other measures of quality of education, for example, in expenditure per student and levels of teachers' salaries (even when adjusted to allow for different levels of living).

A study by the United Nations Research Institute for Social Development attempts to go beyond the limits of educational and economic development, and to set both in a wider framework of social development.[33] The investigators wished to test the hypothesis that "the economic development of countries with a relatively high level of social development [in 1950]—relatively high in comparison with their economic level—would prove to be more rapid in the subsequent period [until 1960]."[34] They collected data for eighteen developing countries between 1950 and 1960 and calculated rank-order correlations between the individual social and economic indicators. Analysis of the data appears to support two

[31] Kaser, "Education and Economic Progress," p. 92.
[32] *Ibid.*, p. 120.
[33] Nancy Baster and Muthu Subramanian, *Aspects of Social and Economic Growth: A pilot statistical study.* Report No. 1. Geneva: United Nations Research Institute for Social Development, Oct. 1965.
[34] *Ibid.*, p. vii. Of the seven indicators of social development used, four are educational: enrollment ratios in primary, secondary, higher, and vocational education.

major conclusions. The first is that the countries in 1950 having what the investigators call a favorable social-economic profile (that is, a relatively high social level in comparison with their economic level) enjoyed more rapid economic growth than countries with an unfavorable social-economic profile. In other words, they find a positive relationship between social levels for 1950 and economic levels in 1960. The second major finding is that "quicker economic growth also seems to have led to relatively greater social growth." Combining these two conclusions provides a picture of complex interaction between social and economic factors.

The specific contribution of such a study clearly does not lie in its conclusions, which previously had been widely recognized in general terms. Rather, it lies in operationalizing the concept of social level and in showing the possibility of using time-lag analysis to clarify causal relationships.[35]

The data included in the *World Handbook of Political and Social Indicators*[36] refer not only to familiar economic and social variables but also include a host of cultural and political indicators brought together in systematic, quantified form.[37] The work of a number of political scientists at Yale University, it employs sophisticated statistical techniques and computer technology to handle awesome masses of numerical data collected from many countries. The compilation presents a modern version of nineteenth-century data-gathering, and is distinguished from earlier works by its emphasis on quantification and careful discussion of the reliability, coverage, and margins of error of the data. It is preoccupied with questions

[35] Further attempts to operationalize such concepts as social growth, social development, and level of living (all of which contain educational components) are reported in subsequent publications of the UNRISD. See Jan Drewnowski, *Social and Economic Factors in Development*, Report no. 3, Geneva: United Nations Research Institute for Social Development, February 1966; and Jan Drewnowski and Wolf Scott, *The Level of Living Index*, Report no. 4, Geneva: United Nations Research Institute for Social Development, September 1966.

[36] Bruce M. Russett, et. al., *World Handbook of Political and Social Indicators*. New Haven: Yale University Press, 1964.

[37] Cf. Arthur S. Banks and Robert B. Textor, *A Cross-Polity Survey*. Cambridge, Mass.: The M.I.T. Press, 1963, which also rates 115 societies with reference to 57 political and social variables, many of which, however, lack the specificity and "objectivity" of the variables used in the *World Handbook*.

of technique and does, in fact, provide much of the data-basis for the first three steps of Bereday's method (description, interpretation, and juxtaposition).

The first part of the book supplies quantitative data on seventy-five variables for over a hundred states and dependencies. Four of these variables deal directly with education—enrollment ratios at different levels of the educational system and literacy rates. The other seventy-one range over indicators of demographic status, communications, wealth, health, religion, and government and politics (the largest single group). Polities are listed in rank order for each variable.

The Handbook provides an invaluable quick reference source and a model of clearly presented data, including frank and (within the limits of space) full discussion of the statistical quirks of each variable. Though the data gathering is guided by no hypotheses, the authors search for clusters of traits that might suggest hypotheses for further study. Nor are the data selected arbitrarily: the authors claim that "Each of the series represents an attempt to operationalize a variable central to several important theories of political or social change."[38]

The second part of the book, in which the data are manipulated, is an analysis of trends and patterns. The results of correlating each of the series with every other series are given; next, the political units are separated into five stages as identified by GNP levels; and for each country in each stage a variety of indicators is given, permitting quantification of such factors as organization, levels of social life, and education. Examination of the way several indicators increase in step with higher levels of GNP per capita strongly suggests the validity of the concept of stages of development. Thus the work supports the contention that, within limits, predictions may be ventured in one sector of a polity if something fairly definite is known about future levels in another sector.

Other techniques of manipulating the data demonstrate ways of quantifying the relative importance of different variables for explaining outcomes. Whereas this may one day lead to statements of

[38] Russett, *op. cit.*, p. 2.

immense value about the causative factors of change and provide a more secure basis for forecasting and planning, the Handbook as it stands is primarily a compendium of quantified and manipulated data.

The scholars associated with this enterprise boldly entered where many others have feared to tread. The twin principles of their faith may be expressed as a conviction that many of the most important questions in social research can be profitably asked and cogently answered only with a framework of cross-national data, and that quantification is the *sine qua non* of cogent answers.[39]

Various kinds of quantitative material are being used to explore specific relationships among selected aspects of social organization and education. Among the topics attracting particular attention are the relation between education and social mobility, the relation between social class background and such educational features as selection and achievement, and the changing social functions of various levels of the school system in response to more general social change.

A number of studies explore the variables that might account for social mobility in different countries. C. Arnold Anderson has questioned the common assumption that education is a dominant factor in accounting for social mobility.[40] The fact that mobility frequently occurs independent of schooling suggests to Anderson that the conventional wisdom requires qualification. He begins with the hypothesis that social status is determined solely by schooling and proceeds to refute it by testing it against the limited data then available. His results, however, indicate that the importance of education varies by social level and country. He concludes that since education is only one important factor it would be valuable to study, step by step, other pertinent correlates such as ability and motivation. However, Fox and Miller, who study the influence of education (as well as per capita national product, po-

[39] Richard L. Merritt and Stein Rokkan (eds.), *Comparing Nations: The Use of Quantitative Data in Cross-National Research,* New Haven: Yale University Press, 1966.

[40] C. Arnold Anderson, "A Skeptical Note on the Relation of Vertical Mobility to Education." *American Journal of Sociology,* **66** (May 1961), 560–570.

litical stability, and urbanization) on certain kinds of mobility, find that education explained 80 per cent of the variance.[41]

Though Fox and Miller's conclusions contradict Anderson's, the two works illustrate the value of limited, highly-structured empirical investigations. Both studies recognize the restricted nature of the data they employ and the problems involved in comparing data from different cultural backgrounds; but both, proceeding from useful middle-range hypotheses concerning the relationship of education and social mobility, provide careful and supportable clarifications of a complex situation in which many variables continually interact. Both works are in the fullest sense heuristic and point the way to improved data gathering and hypothesis testing in the future.

Another interesting attempt to compare education and social mobility in several countries has been made by Robert J. Havighurst.[42] His basic proposition is that "industrialization leads to social change which produces social mobility (group and/or individual) and that education may affect the pace of social change and the degree of social mobility." He makes tentative comparisons of the rates of individual social mobility (both upward and downward) in the United States, England, Australia, and Brazil, and also of group mobility. Speculating about the conditions that produce various kinds of mobility, he details the factors (such as industrialization, differential birth rates, social class structure) in each country that have implications for rates of social mobility. From the countries analyzed, Havighurst derives four models of education that serve to promote mobility under specific conditions.

Four generalizations emerge from this discussion: that there is a great deal of social mobility in an industrial society; that particular conditions encourage individual or group upward mobility; that education has tended to foster mobility; and that different countries make different uses of education in relation to social mobility. Havighurst foresees that "education will be the main instrument for

[41] Thomas G. Fox and S. M. Miller, "Economic, Political and Social Determinants of Mobility: an International Cross-Sectional Analysis," *Acta Sociologica,* **9** (1966), 76–93.

[42] Robert J. Havighurst, "Education, Social Mobility and Social Change in Four Societies," *International Review of Education,* **4** (1958), 168–182.

upward mobility, and lack of education or failure to do well in one's education will be the principal cause of downward mobility."[43] This may indeed be so, but prediction without a clear understanding of the chain of cause and effect is always hazardous, and Havighurst is far from providing an explanation confirmed by systematic testing against data of the precise way education does affect social mobility.

Lipset and Bendix in their book, *Social Mobility and Industrial Society*, review research in education and social mobility as part of a more general study.[44] Like the other empirically-based works discussed, this study is an attempt to consolidate existing empirical data in order to identify testable and important hypotheses. Indeed, a dominant characteristic common to all these works is that they are secondary analyses—studies of specific problems via analysis of data collected for some other purpose.[45]

A unique effort at large-scale primary analysis in comparative education (that is, research based on the collection of original data) has been undertaken by the International Project for the Evaluation of Educational Achievement (IEA). It represents the first attempt on a world-wide basis to measure differences in school achievement, subject by subject, according to internationally agreed upon objective tests and to seek explanations for the differences observed.[46]

The first major publication of the IEA project reports a comparative study of the achievements in mathematics of pupils of secondary school age in twelve industrialized countries.[47] In each country

[43] *Ibid.* p. 182.

[44] Seymour Martin Lipset and Reinhard Bendix, *Social Mobility in Industrial Society.* Berkeley: University of California Press, 1963.

[45] Cf. Robert R. Alford, *Party and Society: the Anglo-American Democracies.* Chicago: Rand McNally, 1963, a comparative study of political attitudes based on existing collections of survey data.

[46] The pilot study is reported in Arthur W. Foshay, et al., *Educational Achievements of Thirteen–Year-Olds in Other Countries.* Hamburg: UNESCO Institute for Education, 1962. Four articles in this volume evaluate the instruments used for gathering preliminary data and begin to propose hypotheses which can already be derived. The authors are especially concerned in this pilot stage with the administrative and methodological problems which further research will face.

[47] Torsten Husén (ed.), *International Study of Achievement in Mathematics: A Comparison of Twelve Countries.* New York: John Wiley, 1967, 2 vols.

tests were administered to representative samples of thirteen-year-olds, and to preuniversity mathematics and nonmathematics students.[48] The final form of the test instruments was agreed upon after extensive scrutiny, discussion, and modification by the international and local specialists. In most participating countries, too, the instruments had been subjected to pretesting. In addition, pupils, teachers, and principals were required to complete extensive questionnaires containing both factual and attitudinal items. Data on school, home, and societal variables were collected, permitting the quantitative expression of relationships between achievement scores of pupils on the one hand and parental, pupil, school, and societal variables on the other. A battery of hypotheses, too extensive to enumerate here, was tested against the data by the use of simple correlation and regression analysis.

The major achievement of the study is to assign to important home, school, and societal variables specific degrees of responsibility for variations in mathematics achievement among and within countries. However, the investigation is not able to account for more than 67 per cent, at the most, of the total variances within a particular population (thirteen-year-olds in the Netherlands); at the least, the study could account for only 23 per cent of the total variance (among preuniversity mathematics students in England). No clear pattern of the importance of given variables appears to explain achievement variance from country to country and from population to population.

Apart from giving a firmer basis for international comparisons of pupil achievement, the findings have some contribution to make to the discussion of major educational controversies and problems: streaming and tracking, comprehensive versus selective secondary schooling, the benefits of traditional versus reformed curricula, coeducation versus single-sex education.

In an ambitious pioneer study of this kind, some weaknesses are inevitable. The administrators of the project had to rely on national organizations in each country to select the samples of pupils tested and to administer the tests and questionnaires. In some countries

[48] Tests were also administered to all pupils in the grade that includes most thirteen-year-olds and some countries gave tests to an intermediate population around age fifteen.

sampling was on a less than scientific basis, and data-gathering procedures were by no means uniform either within or among the countries. Furthermore, the project naturally concentrated on perfecting an original instrument to measure achievement levels; less attention was paid to making measures of inputs from school, home, and society more precise. In addition, great difficulties were encountered in checking the validity of the data supplied from the field, insuring accuracy in recording data, and in casting them into forms suitable for computer-storage and manipulation.

Despite these limitations, one observes marked progress in all respects from the pilot study reported in 1962 to the first completed study reported by Husén: hypotheses are sharpened, variables identified more clearly, sampling within countries improved, and data manipulated and interpreted with greater sophistication.[49] Without doubt, the IEA project is the most impressive piece of empirical comparative research in education yet undertaken. Not only is it an outstanding example of international cooperation, but the data have been collected according to a standardized schema permitting valid comparison. Moreover the results will spur laggards and spread knowledge of new methods. In these ways, the IEA project realizes much of Jullien's dream for the development of comparative education one hundred and fifty years ago; but it goes even further than Jullien's dream—it succeeds in many respects in attaining a high degree of objectivity. Moreover, the researchers recognized that early formulation of hypotheses would be of inestimable value in delimiting the types of data to be collected. From the outset, they were concerned with much more than amassing quantified data and presenting them in comparative tables.

All the work reported on, except that of the IEA, represents the original efforts of social scientists making a contribution to the growth of comparative study in education. In the IEA project,

---

[49] Projected phases of the study will embrace other school subjects and more countries. The national organizations that administered the surveys in individual countries were able to include additional questions relating to particular national problems. It is intended that these separate national studies will be published. At the time of writing only one has appeared, from England: see Douglas A. Pidgeon (ed.), *Achievement in Mathematics: A National Study of Secondary Schools.* London: National Foundation for Educational Research in England and Wales, 1967.

however, the stimulus to cross-national research comes from educators and psychometricians who have enlisted the skills of empirically-oriented social scientists. As a result, preoccupation with scientific methodology emerges as an increasingly dominant theme in this latest stage of comparative research. There is growing readiness and ability to employ the essential elements of scientific method. Heightened recognition is being given to the importance of hypothesis formulation and testing; the concept of controlled investigation through careful selection of cases is being developed; much attention is being paid to precise specification of variables and to quantification of the indicators by which they may be described. Finally, researchers are becoming accustomed to seek quantitatively expressed explanations of the relationships between variables. Through all these elements the explanatory power of comparative research is being sought and advanced.

7

Conclusion

It is now possible to review a century and a half of development and progress since the proposals of Marc-Antoine Jullien de Paris in 1817. This was the period when "pantometry" held sway, indiscriminate measuring was a fad, and hopes were strong that a science of education could emerge from massive collections of data, expressed wherever possible in numerical form.[50] The early quantitative approaches in comparative education failed (as did pantometry in general) partly because they were inappropriately applied, partly because the sources of data and the means of their collection were even more limited than they are today, and finally because the dangers arising from personal and cultural bias were barely recognized.

At that time the failure of primitive quantitative approaches was not crucial since comparative education was directed mainly toward

[50] *Pantometry*—"belief in the possibility of and zeal for extending measurement to all phenomena." See Jacob Viner, "The Economist in History," *American Economic Review*, Papers and Proceedings of the Seventy-fifth Annual Meeting of the American Economic Association (1963), 115.

selective cultural borrowing and was little concerned with the problems of explanation. However, suspicion of statistics persisted even as comparative education moved toward the search for explanation. The qualitative interpretations of Sadler, Kandel, and Hans were magnificent attempts to explain the dynamics of education and society, largely without reference to statistical and quantitative data. From Sadler on, the common approach relied on the identification of forces and factors (*Triebkräfte*) in the search for explanation. Initially, the emphasis was historical; later, sociological, political, and even anthropological factors were introduced. However, the most recent stage in comparative education and cognate fields reverses the classic post-Sadlerian approach: the forces and factors that previously had been the bases for explanation have now themselves become objects of inquiry.

At the same time as the social sciences were developing increasing sophistication in quantification, nonquantitative explanations tended to be ignored. If comparative education was to fulfill its potential as a tool for educational planning, it had to offer a means of reliable prediction. Without a quantitative base, it appeared, this could not be adequately achieved.

In summary, then, during a century and a half comparative education has moved from the stage of curiosity to the stage of analysis. This movement may be discerned along three dimensions: from indiscriminate data gathering to vastly greater precision; from philanthropy in international educational cooperation to professionalism; and from analysis based on intuition toward scientific explanation.

First of all, comparative education has advanced from the stage of curiosity exemplified by Bache's enormous and indiscriminate collections of pedagogical material to the equally vast but now highly-structured collections of data of the IEA project. Second, the early workers in the last century were imbued with humanitarian and philanthropic intentions. They saw the international exchange of educational information as good in itself, but with the exception of Jullien they could not conceive of it as a possible object of conscious, planned, international cooperation. Since the foundation of the International Bureau of Education after World War I, and of Unesco, OECD, and the World Bank after World War II, Jullien's dream has been partially realized. The work of these organizations is in the hands of specialists. Thus, what began with philanthropy has ended with professionalism.

The third and perhaps the most significant dimension along which comparative education has advanced concerns the search for explanation. Early workers were motivated by a vague sense of the differences among nations, an interest in what was going on abroad, and the intention of learning useful lessons. Even when the search for explanations superseded these earlier motivations and when the theories of comparative educators developed comprehensiveness and a sense of the dynamic interrelation of education and society, their approach was largely intuitive. In the most recent phase, a new order of work has appeared in which no explanation can be deemed satisfactory unless validated by rigorous scientific testing.

Part Two

THE METHOD
OF SCIENCE

"Ahem!" said the Mouse with an important air. "Are you all ready? This is the driest thing I know."

8

Introduction:
Ways of Knowing

> *"I ca'n't believe that!" said Alice.*
>
> *"Ca'n't you?" the Queen said in a pitying tone. "Try again: draw a long breath, and shut your eyes."*
>
> *Alice laughed. "There's no use trying," she said: "one ca'n't believe impossible things."*
>
> *"I daresay you haven't had much practice," said the Queen. "When I was your age, I always did it for half-an-hour a day. Why, sometimes I've believed as many as six impossible things before breakfast."*

The first part of this book attempted to trace the quest for explanation based on comparative data. The next task is to examine in detail the empirical, scientific mode of achieving explanation and to indicate the relevance of this approach for comparative education. Whereas the previous part dealt with practice in the field, this section is concerned with the theory of empirical investigation.

Following the paradigm of Charles Peirce, the American pragmatist philosopher, it can be argued that there are four major methods of supporting the validity of statements: by tenacity, authority, intuition, and science.[1] Each of these may be amply illustrated by examples drawn from past work in comparative education, for all investigators using comparative data have justified their beliefs about the nature of the real world and, in particular, their conclusions about the relationships between school and society by employing one or more of these methods.

For example, it has not been uncommon for educational observers to hold tenaciously to the belief that their own institutions and practices are superior to those of foreign nations; many American educators in particular, for a long time assumed that their school system was superior to any other, especially that of the Soviet Union. This belief, rooted in a particular view of the desirable goals for individuals and society, was held tenaciously. Opposing it, unheeded for the most part by American educators, was the view held with equal tenacity by many abroad (including Soviet educators) that their own educational systems were superior. When, during the latter part of the 1950's, American educators began to take Soviet claims of educational superiority into account, the problem arose of reconciling two antithetical sets of beliefs. But tenacity alone could provide no satisfactory answer to the question of whether the American system of education was superior to the Soviet. In this mode of "fixing belief" the very fervor with which assertions are made becomes the measure of their validity. Through constant repetition of a particular assertion, beliefs are reinforced; questioning their validity leads merely to indignant repudiations, which again serve to reinforce the original belief.

A problem arises when a believer in *A* meets a believer in *B* which is incompatible with belief in *A*, for example, when a believer in the superiority of the American system meets a believer in the superiority of the Soviet. If the existence of conflicting views can no longer be brushed aside, the tenacity with which they are held offers no criterion for choosing among them. Nor does it help if one side concedes that it was previously mistaken and that the

[1] See Morris R. Cohen and Ernest Nagel, *An Introduction to Logic and Scientific Method.* New York: Harcourt, Brace, and World, 1934, Chap. X.

other side is correct. In this case, all that has happened is that the old beliefs held on the basis of one's own tenacity are replaced by new beliefs presumably held on the basis of somebody else's tenacity. Comparative education provided an excellent illustration of this particular gambit in the late 1950's and early 1960's. Highly publicized American commentators on education began to assert with great fervor the superiority of European (particularly Soviet) education, but with no sounder basis than earlier spokesmen had when they asserted precisely the reverse.[2]

A second and in some ways far more satisfying method of supporting belief is on the basis of authority. Instead of merely insisting on the truth of one's views and using that very insistence to bolster belief, one appeals to great authorities—religious, tribal, or scholarly and expert. Often we are content to have many issues resolved by an appeal to authority, because we lack the time, desire, or expertise to resolve them ourselves. Prudent reliance on the conclusions already established by authorities can and does form the basis for the expansion of knowledge.

Recourse to authority, however, also has its limitations: difficulties arise in choosing among the conflicting opinions of authorities. There is always the problem of determining the limits of the expertise an authority may properly claim, and in extreme cases the problem may even be to decide who is the authority and who is the charlatan.

Again, some examples from the development of comparative education may be apposite. The entire field has been peculiarly susceptible to the problems arising from reliance on authority. Who has been the expert in comparative education? Often authority has rested on no more solid a basis than travel to the country studied. In other instances it has rested on travel, residence, and knowledge of the language and culture. Sometimes authority in comparative education has even been based on expertise in other fields: teaching, educational administration, politics, or even nuclear engineering.

---

[2] For example, H. G. Rickover, *American Education—A National Failure: The Problem of Our Schools and What We Can Learn from England.* New York: Dutton, 1963; and William Benton, *This Is the Challenge: the Benton Reports of 1956–1958 on the Nature of the Soviet Threat.* Edward W. Barret (ed.). New York: Associated College Presses, 1958.

Where the locus of authority and expertise has not been relevant, appeals to authority have only compounded the difficulties of validating belief.

Comparative education has probably relied most of all on yet a third basis for establishing belief, the method of intuition, which uses "self-evident" propositions as its point of departure. Comparative education, in common with philosophy, science, and mathematics, has shared in the broad intellectual progress that has been achieved on the basis of intuitively revealed truths. But there are two major difficulties arising from this approach. First, one man's self-evident truth may be another's self-evident falsehood. Moreover, one man's self-evident truth may be everyone's, but nevertheless remain false. The history of the progress of human knowledge is littered with the wreckage of such truths that were accepted widely and later refuted. Furthermore, investigations of social phenomena on the basis of self-evident propositions run a special risk of biased reporting of the data: one finds what one seeks. Whatever does not fit the assumptions may not be seen.

Comparative education has had more than its share of errors and problems due to reliance on intuition. For example, the concept of national character has yielded a host of self-evident propositions widely used in comparative analysis. It has been commonly believed by many authors that the behavior of Englishmen demonstrates pragmatism, that of Germans speculative reflection, and that of the French the clear light of reason. Such assumptions about the nature of different peoples are extremely treacherous when they serve to guide investigation into educational systems. The observer is all too apt to find confirmation for his a priori assumption in what he observes. Circular arguments flourish and provide at best only tendentious proof for the original propositions.

On an even wider scale, comparative educators have invited difficulties when they have begun their investigations from the "self-evident" proposition that a nation's educational system is a product of its historical traditions—by no means an unreasonable assumption. But difficulty has arisen when the investigator has used the "facts" of history to explain the present, for only the elements in the past that are seen to contribute to the formation of the present may come to be acknowledged as historical facts. The resulting circularity in argument has weakened the conclusions. This is not to say that the method of intuition is without value. Indeed, the intuitively based insight of the investigator frequently is the starting point of fruitful study in the sciences. It is, however, necessary that propositions based on intuition be constantly validated empirically, that is, by the evidence of the real world.

A beginning is, indeed, being made in the systematic testing of some of the more common a priori propositions in comparative education. For example, in the pilot report of the IEA Project, it was suggested that one hypothesis for investigation might be: "National groups show consistent differences in willingness to express certainty about a conclusion."[3] Thus what earlier investigators would have taken for granted about national character was offered as a subject for validation.[4]

Each of the three methods of substantiating knowledge or belief just discussed has been widely used to achieve intellectual progress in general and to substantiate statements in comparative education in particular. But comparative education is peculiarly susceptible to the basic problems of bias and lack of generally accepted criteria for belief inherent in each of these methods. None is free from these problems. None of them, as Cohen and Nagel point out, is free from human caprice and willfulness.[5] None of them has self-correcting devices to prevent error even though the presence of error may be fully recognized. Ideally, what is required is a method of inquiry that is self-correcting, that minimizes the possibility of observer bias and maximizes the validity of data. Above all, it must be a method that opens to public scrutiny each step of the investigation and the logical and empirical bases for the researcher's conclusions. All this points towards what has come to be known as the method of science.

[3] A. Foshay, et al., *Educational Achievements of Thirteen Year Olds in Other Countries,* Hamburg: UNESCO Institute for Education, 1962, p. 40.

[4] The report of Phase 1 of the IEA Project takes this approach even further. It discusses the possibility of translating national style or character into specific, identifiable educational practices and relating variations in these educational practices to variations in educational output, in this case, mathematics achievement. See Torsten Husén (ed.), *International Study of Achievement in Mathematics: A Comparison of Twelve Countries.* New York: John Wiley, 1967, vol. 1, pp. 71–72.

[5] Cohen and Nagel, *op. cit.,* p. 195.

9

Scientific Method
and the Study of Society

> *The White Rabbit put on his spectacles. "Where shall I begin, please your Majesty?" he asked.*
> *"Begin at the beginning," the King said, very gravely, "and go on till you come to the end: then stop."*

A central advantage of the scientific method is that it offers a consistent way of dealing with problems of bias, tendentiousness, and even caprice and willfulness. All facts and propositions are approached with skepticism, but the method goes beyond mere persistent and corrosive doubt, offering a technique for combining belief with skepticism. From skepticism about the facts flows the continual attempt in science to improve instruments of observation and data gathering. From skepticism about propositions flows the practice of continually testing deductively based arguments against the facts of the real world. This combination of inductive and deductive thought is, moreover, progressive in the sense that knowledge is perceived to be an open-end system: the conclusions of one stage of inquiry suggest the questions for subsequent investigation.

Thus, the method of science embodies two features: a characteristic attitude and a characteristic research strategy. The scientific attitude toward what constitutes the firm establishment of knowledge about social phenomena has been described in the following manner:

> The social scientist no longer assumes that the facts of social or po- litical life are known, or that they are easily accessible through casual observation, introspection, or systematic reading. One questions not merely the interpretation of facts, but in the first instance the facts themselves. Most important, perhaps, the criteria by which one accepts or rejects statements about social life are of a special nature. The ulti- mate criterion is the method by which they are gathered. The method should be relatively systematic and relatively reliable. And it ought to be amenable to replication, so that some other researcher looking at the same body of material would come up with roughly the same facts. Of course all this implies that the method be public and explicit.[1]

This new attitude in the social sciences is inseparably bound up with a research strategy that is scientific, that is, "systematic, con- trolled, empirical, and critical."[2]

The word systematic refers to the orderly statement of the problem to be investigated and the procession through the logical steps required to solve it. The particular steps involved in solving any given problem and their relation to one another depend, of course, on the nature of the problem and the kinds of data. Yet the general shape of these procedures does not vary. Scientific research begins in the mind of the investigator, very often with an indefinite sense that a problem exists. At this stage the question may be vague and inchoate; the investigator is uncertain about its precise nature, but motivated by curiosity and guided by intuition, he attempts to refine the problem so that it may be opened to more exact examina- tion. At this point he is defining the field in which the problem exists,

[1] Gabriel A. Almond and Sidney Verba, *The Civic Culture: Political At- titudes and Democracy in Five Nations.* Princeton, N.J.: Princeton University Press, 1963, p. 43.
[2] Fred N. Kerlinger, *Foundations of Behavioral Research.* New York: Holt, Rinehart and Winston, 1965, p. 13.

collecting information within this relatively limited field and refining the concepts that will enable him to state the problem. These activities do not necessarily take place sequentially; it is much more likely that they will occur contemporaneously. In any event, what emerges is some tentative hypothesis or group of hypotheses that is then employed to review the problems, data, and concepts. The work now consists of defining the problem and refining the data and concepts. The investigator's object is to use ever more focused data to test the validity of increasingly precise hypotheses. This systematic procedure aims at the progressive discarding of unsatisfactory hypotheses and the substitution of more satisfactory ones. The investigator's task is, for the moment, completed when he arrives at hypotheses he is unable to reject, given the state of his data and techniques of analysis.[3]

The word "control" in the definition of scientific research does not have the same meaning as it does in everyday usage; that is, it does not imply simply the guidance, administration, and ordering of research activity. Instead, it has a very special and important connotation: guarding against the adulteration of results by extraneous factors. Control of an observation or experiment seeks to isolate variables so that the influence of extraneous factors, especially chance, can be confidently ruled out. It is this combination of systematic and controlled procedures that permits investigators to have critical confidence in the results they obtain.[4]

Scientific research is by definition both empirical and critical. It is empirical in insisting on the constant checking of ideas against data, whether these ideas spring from intuitive knowledge or from previously validated findings. Validation is constantly sought outside the investigator. It is critical because it is founded not only on habitual skepticism, but on a method that contains a series of self-correcting checks at all stages. These checks are implicit in a research strategy that is systematic, controlled, and empirical.

[3] John Dewey, *How We Think,* Boston: Heath, 1933, pp. 106–118; and Mark A. May in the foreword to J. Dollard, et al., *Frustration and Aggression,* New Haven: Yale University Press, 1939, pp. vii–viii.

[4] Fred N. Kerlinger, *Foundations of Behavioral Research.* New York: Holt, Rinehart and Winston, 1965, p. 13.

Hypothesis

"It's too late to correct it," said the Red Queen: "when you've once said a thing, that fixes it, and you must take the consequences."

The scientific method embraces not only the characteristics of the scientific approach, but also a very special concern for the hypothesis. All efforts at data gathering, classification, manipulation, and interpretation are directed toward testing the validity of hypotheses, which are, in fact, the key to scientific procedure. A hypothesis is defined as a statement asserting a presumed relation among natural phenomena.[5] As such, it calls for a conclusion in which one set of phenomena is expressed as a function of another. In its simplest form this is a statement of the type: "As x changes, so y changes."

Such functional statements are the common stuff of certain important branches of mathematics and have come to be exceptionally useful in the social sciences, where the interactions of phenomena are studied. In mathematics, to assert that y is a function of x means that the value of y is dependent on the value of x. Of course this is not to say that the change in y will necessarily be exactly proportional to the change in x over the entire range of the observed values of x. It may be more or less than proportional. The numerical value of the relationship can easily change from one value of x to another. Thus, the relationship between x and y may be linear (constant and proportional) or nonlinear (nonproportional) over different sections of the range. This type of formulation of a functional relationship between dependent and independent variables is extremely useful in the social sciences generally and in the study of education in particular. Changes in educational variables often are believed to be dependent on changes in identifiable variables inside the school or in the wider society. Thus, elements in the economy, the social structure, politics, and the culture are com-

[5] *Ibid.*, p. 30.

monly isolated as affecting what the schools look like and what goes on inside them.

This mathematical view of function leads inevitably to the formulation of increasingly precise statements about the relationship between dependent and independent variables. The comparative educator, for example, may seek to investigate the relationship he suspects to exist between political totalitarianism and authoritarian discipline in classrooms. At the simplest level he would like to determine whether such a relationship does exist. At a more sophisticated level, he would like to know the direction of the relationship; that is, he considers a proposition such as "the more totalitarian the political system, the more authoritarian the classroom." This offers a more refined definition of the functional relationship under study. But it is a third, and even more sophisticated, level of investigation that promises to lend greater precision to the conclusion, one in which quantification is crucial. Here the researcher seeks to measure the relation between politics and classroom climate over a range of the two variables and seeks to make statements of the type: increase of the totalitarianism of a society up to a certain point leads to a large increase in authoritarianism within the classroom; further increase in political totalitarianism over a middle range affects the classroom climate to a very limited degree; and increase in the higher ranges of political totalitarianism leads to a great increase in authoritarianism in classrooms. In other words, the researcher seeks to establish first the existence of the relationship, second its general direction, and third a more precise and preferably quantified statement of the relationship.

It is of course a giant step to move from the first stage, in which a functional relationship is either merely asserted (or denied) to the third stage. It amounts to moving from a formulation in symbolic terms to fleshing out the symbols with numbers describing phenomena that in many cases have never previously been counted.

It is, moreover, important to distinguish between the mathematical sense of the concept of function and the way it has been commonly employed in the social sciences. Certain sociologists and anthropologists have regarded institutions (including education) as fulfilling a set of common functions or tasks in their social contexts. According to these theorists, study of the structures of social institutions must be supplemented by study of their functions. Furthermore, they have claimed that institutions located in different societies can be validly compared if they perform common functions, regardless of their superficial differences. The development of this functional approach has permitted anthropologists, for example, to compare total cultures by reference to the ways they satisfy needs common to all humanity. Whereas the use of this concept of function may help in the comparative analysis of education, the mathematical sense is more relevant to the current discussion.[6]

A statement of a functional relationship is one that refers to covariation.[7] It need not necessarily refer to causal relationships, even though intimations of causality may be embedded in the statement. For example, an investigator might discover that educational levels (literacy rates, enrollment figures, and so on) are high in capitalistic economic systems and low in precapitalist ones. Even if this is so, the finding does not necessarily mean that the one causes the other, but merely that they covary. In cases like this, the investigator might postulate a single anterior cause of both covarying phenomena, which in turn will require further research. For example, if he accepts the Weber/Tawney thesis, the investigator might hypothesize that Protestantism is the anterior cause of both capitalist economic organization and high educational levels.

There is another sense in which a functional statement may fail to explain a relationship satisfactorily. It may not reveal the direction of influence from one factor to another. Thus, even when one is able to show that educational levels and levels of economic

[6] For discussion of the limitations of the functional approach in comparative education, see Andreas M. Kazamias and Byron G. Massialas, *Tradition and Change in Education: a Comparative Study*. Englewood Cliffs, N.J.: Prentice Hall, 1965, pp. 10–13. On the dangers of comparative and functional studies, see David E. Apter, *The Politics of Modernization*. Chicago: University of Chicago Press, 1965, pp. 423–434. For an early statement of the functional approach in anthropology, see Bronislaw Malinowski, *A Scientific Theory of Culture and Other Essays*. New York: Oxford University Press, 1960, pp. 147–176. For a critical refutation of the functional approach, see Kingsley Davis, "The Myth of Functional Analysis as a Special Method in Sociology and Anthropology," *American Sociological Review*, **24** (December 1959), 757–772.

[7] See S. F. Nadel, *The Foundations of Social Anthropology*. London: Cohen and West, 1951, Chapter IX, pp. 222–256, for a discussion of "the method of covariations."

development vary systematically, it may be difficult to determine whether it is the educational level that affects economic development, or vice-versa.

There is yet another limitation inherent in bare functional statements. Assuming that covariation is established and that the statement incorporates a clear formulation of cause-and-effect relationships, the precise mechanism by which x causes y may still remain unstated. Here the inputs into the process are defined, and so are the outputs, but the process that connects the two goes forward in the obscurity of a "black box," the mysteries of which have not been revealed. For example, a great deal of evidence has been accumulated that under certain circumstances more education causes economic levels in a nation to rise. But the exact ways this takes place remain to be discovered, and generally, statements expressing causal relationships are extremely difficult to validate.

Thus, to summarize the argument so far, functional statements may show no more than covariation; and, if they do show covariation, they may not reveal the direction of the influence between factors; and even when the direction is known, the mechanism of the relationship between cause and effect may remain obscure. Although all this may sound somewhat pessimistic, the functional approach is the only way to extend knowledge of relationships among phenomena. On the basis of functional statements, systematically tested and cumulated, it is possible to extrapolate from the past to the present, thus providing at the very least a way of explaining how the past has generated the present.

The value of hypotheses, expressed as functional statements, is not limited, however, to their potential for clarifying relationships among phenomena. Hypotheses also are crucial for giving direction to an investigation; they serve as guides to the accumulation and manipulation of data.

From a scientific point of view it is misleading to assume that facts in the sense of undifferentiated data have any meaning or significance. A datum becomes a fact to be taken into account only when it is deliberately sought out, classified, and inserted into a context. The context includes other facts, relationships among those facts, and consequences. An historical item becomes a fact of history, E. H. Carr has observed, when, and only when, the historian selects it and places it with other items in a context of explanation.[8] Thus, the wart on Cromwell's nose only becomes a historical fact when a historian selects it for use in an historical description or explanation. For the investigator, the volume of educational items, like that of historical items, is overwhelming. Everywhere governments and other organizations discharge torrents of educational information, statistical and other. None of these items can become educational facts in the sense just defined unless they are deliberately selected and placed in context with a view to explanation. Without a hypothesis, the investigator is in danger of wandering aimlessly in an uncharted jungle of data. Armed with one, he possesses a guide to the selection of some data and the rejection of the rest.

The necessity for a hypothesis may be illustrated by an example from comparative education. Take the hypothesis, "educational discrimination against minority groups decreases as industrialization increases." Immediately the field of investigation for the researcher is limited and focused. He may now ignore broad tracts of educational and social data that do not bear on the subjects of educational discrimination, minority groups, and industrialization. This is not to say that decisions concerning relevance are always easy. Very often they are not. But the great virtue of a guiding hypothesis is that it forces the investigator to consider which data are to be immediately brought into the study, which are to be completely and absolutely excluded, and which are to be held in abeyance for the time being, pending further decision.

It is important to recognize that there normally exists what might be termed "tension" between data and hypothesis. The hypothesis to be tested determines the types of data collected and the uses made of them. Conversely, the kinds of data available determine the types of hypotheses that can be reasonably postulated and practically tested. Whether it is even possible to investigate a given hypothesis depends on the kinds of data available; but also, if the data are not available, or are grossly inadequate, postulating a

[8] E. H. Carr, *What Is History?* New York: Alfred A. Knopf, 1962.

hypothesis may stimulate the production of data that previously did not exist.

It is not only inefficient and uneconomical to enter the data without a hypothesis, but in an important sense it is not fair:

> . . . use of the hypothesis is similar to playing a game of chance. The rules of the game are set up in advance. . . . One cannot change the rules after an outcome, nor can one change one's bets after making them. That would not be "fair." One cannot throw the dice first and then bet. Similarly, if one gathers data first and then selects a datum and comes to a conclusion on the basis of the datum, one has violated the rules of the scientific game.[9]

These are by no means mere formal rules, for violating them opens the door to the possibility of serious error. Assume that the investigator examines some data and without any particular hypothesis in mind arranges them in categories. Perhaps he notices that there are some correlations between one set of data and another and he may be tempted to go on to assert that there is a relationship between the two. There is always a chance that the relationship is meaningful, but it is equally or perhaps more likely that there are other important relationships that have been missed because of limitations on the part of the observer or in the data. Even more treacherous may be the appearance of quite spurious relationships. The facts must be given a chance to do as much as possible, and they can do this only in conjunction with a previously formulated hypothesis.

To illustrate further, perhaps an investigator, innocent of any explicit hypothesis, collects information about English and German secondary education and arranges it in common-sense categories: the age at which pupils generally leave school, the subjects they study, the length of time they study, curriculum content, levels of achievement, the training of the teachers, and so on. On scrutiny, perhaps, two features leap out of the comparative tables: German children are generally older than English children when they leave secondary school and on average their academic achievement is higher. The investigator who has collected data without any hypothesis in mind can only assert a relationship between age of com-

---

[9] Kerlinger, *op. cit.*, p. 24.

pleting school and level of achievement. He has not even begun to prove it. Moreover, he may be observing only a spurious relationship and missing valid ones.

Such dangers cannot be avoided merely by broadening the scope of the study to include more data and more countries. Perhaps in an expanded study, after arranging his data on secondary education the same way as before, the investigator now notes that there is a positive relationship between the age of leaving secondary school and academic achievement in many of the countries. If he then asserts that the relationship exists, he is in effect simply ignoring the cases that do not support him. It is as if he were betting after the dice had been rolled. Thus, collection and categorization of data are not sufficient bases for explanation, let alone proof. Facts alone prove nothing. They require the prior formulation of a hypothesis if they are to work for the investigator. They also require translation into a language that facilitates the most effective testing of the hypothesis, and this calls for data to be cast in quantified form.

Quantification

> "Oh, don't bother me!" said the Duchess. "I never could abide figures!"

While the primacy of hypotheses has been urged thus far, the data clearly have a great claim to attention. The data in the real world provide the objective evidence against which all hypothesized relationships must be tested. The observer of social phenomena too often is subjective. Only the data are neutral. Yet the neutral data must be arranged and handled and consequently transformed if they are to acquire meaning within an investigation, and both the researcher and the test of the hypothesis are highly vulnerable to bias. Quantitative methods applied to data handling and testing a presumed relationship between phenomena help maintain objectivity.

A quantitative approach is, in fact, forced upon the scientific investigator who, even as a bare minimum, wishes to establish only the presence or absence of the phenomena indicated by the hypothesis. At a slightly more sophisticated level, questions of more or less arise. Concern about the extent to which phenomena are or are not present is inherent in most statements about a presumed relationship. Hence there is constant inducement to go beyond simple binary scales indicating the presence or absence of phenomena and to construct scales for ranking phenomena according to the extent (that is, intensity or frequency) to which they are present.

It is often desirable to do more than merely rank phenomena along some relevant dimension and assert a general more or less statement. Greater precision may be necessary and this is achieved by specifying how much more or how much less. Thus there is a progression from a simple binary (yes/no) scale through an ordinal (ranking) scale, and then on to a cardinal (how much?) scale. Each step in the progression represents a superior form of quantification: it enables more information to be conveyed with more precision about the phenomena.

There is a common belief that quantification is severely limited in its application. It is indeed true that many kinds of data do not appear to be very amenable to cardinal quantification, but binary and ordinal scales are also a form of quantification, if somewhat less sophisticated. Even in apparently nonquantitative studies, primitive quantitative measures have, in fact, usually been applied to qualitative factors. For example, in studying the relationship between democratic forms of government and education, comparative educators have been forced to decide at the very least whether democracy has been present or not in a given country. Further, if they wished to make comparisons between countries, they have had to be concerned often with the extent to which democratic forms were present in each.

There is, moreover, a tendency to consider quantification as no more than "nose counting." But cardinal measurement is not limited in its uses to counting discrete and concrete objects, for it is commonly applied to far less tangible phenomena. Many cardinal measures frequently used in daily life are artificial constructs. Thus, when we look at a thermometer and see that the temperature is 68°, it does not concern us unduly that the Fahrenheit degrees of temperature are not natural objects, but elements of an artificial scale created by physicists.

In comparative education, the use of numbers is conventional for such purposes as measuring the size of school enrollment, but explicit attempts to quantify tend to be rejected in other matters. For example, when comparative educators consider classroom discipline or curriculum emphasis, they tend to shun quantification, asserting that these matters are best handled without recourse to numbers. However, because qualitative comparisons of the type "more authoritarian—less authoritarian classrooms" or "more academic—less academic curricula" are inevitable, quantitative measures really cannot be avoided. They are implicit in the description of the variables. In fact, the very nature of the comparative method in education, as in other social science inquiry, demands that investigators make every effort to quantify explicitly rather than covertly.

The expression of phenomena by figures and symbols allows a large number to be compared simultaneously, their respective characteristics can be set against one another with great accuracy, and their analysis taken much further. In striving to introduce "quantification" and mathematics into their disciplines as far as possible, specialists in the social sciences, contrary to what many laymen think, are not merely deferring to a fashion, but are recognizing that mathematics provides analytical tools incomparably more effective than classical comparative methods.[10]

Yet satisfactory quantification of data is not easily achieved. For one thing there are always limits to the precision with which even the simplest phenomena can be quantitatively expressed. Errors inevitably creep into even the apparently simple tasks of educational enumeration, such as counting school enrollments, so that demand for total precision is always unrealistic. The job of the investigator is to allow for error, and, if he can achieve any control over the collection of data in the future, to try to narrow the error progressively. Even in the most precise sciences, errors of measure-

[10] Maurice Duverger, *Introduction to the Social Sciences* (translated by M. Anderson) London: Allen and Unwin, 1964, p. 277.

ment are not only expected, they are tolerated. Thus, the physicist does not have a completely accurate measure of the velocity of light, one of the most important physical constants with which he deals. But he recognizes that in his calculations he must make allowance for probable error.[11] Moreover, in the social sciences in particular, even the simplest counting procedures take time. During the interval of counting, change may take place in the phenomenon being measured so that the final result is unreliable as a completely accurate measure.

More serious than these problems, which arise out of imperfections of instruments, is the willful misrepresentation of data by a variety of vested interests. Governments, respondents to questionnaires, and educational administrators all may have reasons for not reporting accurately. Considerations of national prestige enter into reporting of literacy statistics and grants of aid from central authorities often depend on figures of school enrollment. Thus, there may be advantages to be gained by inflated reporting, and when data are deliberately misrepresented it is exceptionally difficult to estimate the margin of error.

Another fundamental difficulty arises when scales are constructed for measuring qualitative differences among, for example, school curricula. Assume that a comparative educator wishes to rank countries on a curriculum scale that runs from subject-centered to child-centered. A curriculum is composed of different school subjects, each of which is assessed separately. The individual subject assessments must then be pooled to form an aggregate curriculum assessment for each country. But how does one aggregate, say, a highly subject-centred mathematics curriculum with a highly child-centered language curriculum in one country? Presumably the technique of weighting may provide an answer. But the choice of weights is critical. The separate subjects that make up the total curriculum must be weighed according to some defensible criteria. If the same set of weights can be used for all countries (which is

---

[11] Regrettably it is still not customary to attach probable margins of error to social statistics when quoting them. Failure to do so often lends a false appearance of accuracy to data which are, at best, judicious estimates and, at worst, pure guesses. See Oskar Morgenstern, *On the Accuracy of Economic Observations,* second edition. Princeton, N.J.: Princeton University Press, 1963, pp. 8–9.

by no means always possible), simple ranking of the curricula along the scale may be feasible. But a further problem arises. The investigator often wishes to know not only that country A has a more subject-centered curriculum than country B, but by how much it is different and whether in any sense an absolute difference of, say, ten points between A and B at the lower end of the scale can be compared with an absolute difference of ten points between countries C and D at the upper end. Allotting absolute values to intervals along such a scale is a problem that remains intractable more often than not.

There are, without doubt, some difficult theoretical and practical problems in the use of quantified data. Perfect accuracy is always impossible to achieve. To the uninitiated, numbers may lend data an authority that is wholly spurious. More serious still is the temptation simply to concentrate on what is easily and obviously measurable, to the neglect of phenomena that are inherently difficult to quantify, or for which measuring instruments do not exist. Yet all attempts at quantification are attempts to increase precision and objectivity in description and explanation. Quantification provides a continual incentive to make more precise the definition of terms and increases the possibilities of manipulating data. But probably the most important dividend to be gained from the use of quantitative technique is that it permits conclusions to be stated in a form that specifies how much confidence can be placed in them.

Control

The shop seemed to be full of all manner of curious things—but the oddest part of it all was that, whenever she looked hard at any shelf, to make out exactly what it had on it, that particular shelf was always quite empty, though the others round it were crowded as full as they could hold.

"Things flow about so here!" [Alice] said at last in a plaintive tone . . .

In the natural sciences, when an investigator observes interesting differences in the behavior of, say, electrons or living cells, he is usually able to devise experiments that give him the chance to isolate and identify the factors causing the differences. Most frequently he will employ the method of controlled experimentation. In this procedure the investigator sets up his experiments as far as possible to isolate the effect of varying one and only one clearly identified factor in the total situation, *all other factors remaining constant.* For example, a biologist wishing to investigate the effect on crop yield of adding a certain chemical to the soil sets up a controlled experiment in which some plants receive the chemical additive while others, as nearly alike in all other respects, do not. The results are carefully compared, with particular attention paid to the elimination of purely chance factors, before the conclusions are formulated.

In the social sciences, including the study of educational systems, little if any controlled experimentation is possible. People object to being subjects of experimentation, however nobly intended; experimental time periods must usually be reckoned in years, if not in decades; and the very act of experimentation is likely to affect the attitudes and behavior of the subjects, a complication that casts doubt on the validity of the findings. Moreover, in the social sciences, even if experiment is possible, it can only be performed once: as soon as a particular experiment is completed, the nature of the data is changed, usually irreversibly. Consequently a second attempt at the same experiment with the same data is rarely possible.

However, if the prospects for controlled experimentation in the social sciences are necessarily poor, the same is not true of the prospects for controlled *investigation*. Controlled investigation is, in essence, the comparative method.[12] It is used extensively even in some of the natural sciences (for example, astronomy) where experimentation may be ruled out by the nature of the material studied. By careful choice of comparable situations, the investigator seeks to isolate the effect on the phenomena of variations in identi-

[12] See Ernest Nagel, *The Structure of Science: Problems in the Logic of Scientific Explanation.* New York: Harcourt, Brace, and World, 1961; particularly Chapters 13 and 14.

fied factors. After many such controlled investigations he tries to make a general statement about the way a specific factor works. Although such general statements cannot be tested by experimentation, they may be used for predictions, which may then be checked either against future outcomes or against missing parts of the present.[13]

In comparative education, similarly, general statements may be sought and validated by their predictive value in these two senses. Thus, the United States educational system is noted for unevenness of the quality of school provision from state to state and even within states. If it is hypothesized that this is a result of lack of central administration of education, other large educational systems, such as those in the Soviet Union, China, Australia, Canada, and Indonesia, may be investigated in order to test the hypothesis. Suppose it is concluded that the hypothesis is valid: that lack of central supervision coincides with uneven standards of school provision. It may then be predicted that if increased centralization of education in the United States occurs (most observers seem to expect it), the result will be a narrowing of the gap between the quality of education provided in the best states and the worst ones, and between the best districts inside individual states and the worst ones. If the prediction is confirmed at the end of the next decade it will reinforce confidence in the value of the general statement that prompted the prediction. Validation of the hypothesis may be sought also by testing its predictive value against contemporary situations in other countries so far excluded from the sample. If the degree of centralization can predict the degree of unevenness of school provision in these additional cases, then missing parts of the present have been successfully predicted. This will not prove the general statement beyond doubt; it is always possible to be right for the wrong reasons. But the more consistently a general statement helps to make correct predictions in both senses of the word, the more confidence can be placed in it.

Controlled experimentation and controlled investigation appear

[13] See Daniel Bell, "Twelve Modes of Prediction" in *Penguin Survey of the Social Sciences, 1965,* edited by Julius Gould. Harmondsworth, Middlesex: Penguin Books, 1965.

to be alternative methods of scientific inquiry. Whether the researcher manipulates the variables himself or whether nature has done this for him implies the existence of only procedural and not logical differences between the two. The nature of the field to be investigated determines whether controlled experimentation or controlled investigation will predominate. This principle does not require controlled experimentation to be the characteristic method of the physical sciences and controlled investigation to be the characteristic method of the social sciences. In the physical sciences, as already pointed out, researchers often are unable to make use of controlled experimentation and must be satisfied with controlled investigation; moreover, in some restricted areas of the behavioral sciences (particularly in psychology) controlled experimentation is frequently employed.

Theory

> *"What do you know about this business?"* the King said to Alice.
> *"Nothing,"* said Alice.
> *"Nothing* whatever?" *persisted the King.*
> *"Nothing whatever,"* said Alice.

In order to avoid the dangers of advancing hypotheses at random, it is highly desirable to root hypotheses in theory.

Theory is more important in cross-national research than in any other field. When doing national studies or studies of narrow subjects, the researcher may have hunches about the validity of his indicators or operational definitions. He is able to assess the face validity of his indicators. In comparative research, in which many and greatly varying environments are compared, it is not humanly possible to have hunches about the face validity of all the indicators. Unless the researcher in cross-national research has a theory or some system of hypotheses which guide him, he will almost assuredly encounter a situation in which he regards as similar phenomena which are actually different and which measure different things.[14]

A hypothesis itself does not constitute a theory. The former is a much more limited type of statement in the sense that it is an assertion about a particular relationship that is presumed to exist between delimited phenomena. Theory is formed from an inter-related set of hypotheses; at the same time, developing theory suggests new hypotheses for testing. Through these two intercon-nected processes, the heuristic benefits of empirical method are gained.

The play of speculation and the logical processes of reason have a large part in the formulation of theory. Initial browsing among the data stimulates the researcher to formulate problems, and to attempt solutions. One approach is deductive reasoning. This in-volves establishing a number of "self-evident propositions" and reasoning from them according to accepted canons of logic. For example, the investigator observes the rigor of German academic programs and the strict discipline permeating the classrooms in the *Gymnasien* and explains these characteristics by referring to the well-known predilection of the German people for firm discipline, arguing from this that it characterizes all aspects of German society, including the schools.

But the arbitrary imposition of a set of preconceived generaliza-tions usually fails to provide adequate proof. Of course it may be absolutely true that one can explain discipline inside German schools by reference to the alleged characteristic love of discipline among the German people. The difficulty is that deductive methods alone provide no way of proving it adequately. What is needed is the empirical testing of the basic propositions about the nature of the German people, the influence of that character on the society in general and the schools in particular, and the proof that this element of the German national character, rather than anything else, is at the root of the educational phenomenon observed. More-over, if proof of the influence of German national character on the

[14] Erik Allardt, "Implications of Within-Nation Variations and Regional Imbalances for Cross-National Research," in Merritt and Rokkan, *Com-paring Nations: The Use of Quantitative Data in Cross-National Research.* New Haven: Yale University Press, 1966, p. 348.

schools is indeed obtained, parts of a more general theory are constructed about the influence of national character on education. Any statements that are now made on the basis of such a wider theory must, of course, be subject to empirical testing. If they are confirmed, the theory is substantiated to that extent; if disconfirmed, the theory must be modified. Thus, deductive and inductive reasoning play alternate and equally important roles in the construction of imaginative and sound theory. Deduction helps in identifying the problem, locating it within the framework of a broader theory, and devising hypotheses. Induction restrains us from spinning cocoons of logically impeccable but empirically untestable arguments and theories.

Theory may be regarded as a map that investigators are trying to construct, a symbolic picture of the locational relationships between places.[15] Scientific research based on hypotheses helps test certain presumed relationships between places on the map. As some hypotheses are rejected and others provisionally accepted, the map (that is, the theory) gains in detail and accuracy. The aim is to form a unified, cumulative body of empirical evidence.

There are two main views on the value of organizing bodies of tested hypotheses into theory. The first emphasizes explanation and understanding. This may be regarded as the pure scientific approach, as distinct from the applied. The second approach, which may be called the instrumental view, holds that scientific theory aims at prediction and the possibility of control. The immediate goal of scientific knowledge is the power consciously to influence outcomes. Again, perhaps the best analogy is with map-making. Consider the difference between a map and a route, or between a map-maker and a route-marker. A map is purpose- (and route-) neutral. It is a symbolic picture of the general location relationships between places. It *can* be used for route-marking, but that is not its only (or even its prime) function.

Applying empirical methods to test hypotheses and formulate theory in comparative education is an attempt to construct a "map" of relationships between education and society. Such maps,

[15] On the analogy between theory and maps, see Stephen Toulmin, *The Philosophy of Science—An Introduction.* New York: Harper and Row, 1960, chap. 4.

or theories, need not have any direct instrumental uses. However, empirical methods in comparative education can also be regarded as the equivalent of route-marking on maps, for they have very special practical applications. Thus, questions may be asked that imply analysis of causes with a view to guiding change: "Why did the plan for Indian educational development fail?" "Why is there a shortage of teachers in Nigeria?" "Why do Uzbek children leave school earlier than Russian children?" This type of analysis is an essential part of the work of the applied scientist, but it has little or no place in the work of the pure scientist, who is much more interested in establishing general relationships than in investigating causes of particular phenomena. He will not ask "Why did the plan for Indian educational development fail?" but "What are the conditions for the success of educational plans?"; and not "Why is there a shortage of teachers in Nigeria?" but "What are the factors affecting the supply of and demand for teachers?"

There is widespread contemporary recognition of the utility of scientific method in the social sciences; witness much of the current work in anthropology, economics, sociology, political science, and economic history.[16] For example, in sociology the introduction to Dahrendorf's *Class and Class Conflict in Industrial Society* contains a strong assertion of the commonality of scientific method to both the physical and the social sciences.

If in this study I speak of "theory," "hypothesis," "empirical test," "refutation," and "science," I use these terms in the strict sense of the

[16] For example, Gideon Sjoberg, "The Comparative Method in the Social Sciences," *Philosophy of Science*, **22** (April 1955). Gabriel A. Almond and Sidney Verba, *The Civic Culture: Political Attitudes and Democracy in Five Nations*. Princeton, N.J.: Princeton University Press, 1963; Gabriel A. Almond and James S. Coleman (eds.), *The Politics of the Developing Areas*. Princeton: Princeton University Press, 1960, pp. 3–64. James C. Charlesworth (ed.), *Mathematics and the Social Sciences: The Utility and Inutility of Mathematics in the Study of Economics, Political Science, and Sociology*. Philadelphia: The American Academy of Political and Social Science, 1963; James C. Charlesworth (ed.), *A Design for Political Science: Scope, Objectives, and Methods*. (Monograph 6); Philadelphia: The American Academy of Political and Social Science, 1966; Bruce Russett, et al., *World Handbook of Political and Social Indicators*. New Haven: Yale University Press, 1964; Ralf Dahrendorf, *Class and Class Conflict in Industrial Society*. Stanford: Stanford University Press, 1959; Lance Davis, "Professor Fogel and the New Economic History," *The Economic History Review*, **29** (December 1966), 657–663.

methodological characteristics of an empirical discipline. At least logically, physics, physiology, and sociology are subject to the same laws —whatever may render one or the other of these disciplines empirically preferable in terms of exactness. I cannot see why it should not be at least desirable to try to free sociology of the double fetters of an idiographic historical and a meta-empirical philosophical orientation and weld it into an exact social science with precisely—ideally, of course, mathematically—formulated postulates, theoretical models, and testable laws. The attempt must be made; and although the present study remains far removed from its satisfactory completion, I want it to be understood in terms of such an attempt.[17]

In the field of historical analysis, too, the approach through controlled investigation has found its proponents. What the "new history" purports to do is,

First to state precisely the questions subject to examination and to define operationally the relevant variables. Second, to build explicit models that are relevant to the questions at hand. Third, to produce evidence (frequently quantitative, but at times qualitative) of the world as it actually existed. And finally, to test the model (a logical statement of assumptions and conclusions) against the evidence (the world that did exist) and the counterfactual deduction (the world that did not exist).[18]

It would be quite wrong to assume from these strong expressions of support for the empirical approach that all previous studies, especially of historical analysis of particular cases, were without merit. At its best, the earlier work has excelled in its careful definition of concepts, evaluation of evidence, and statement of conclusions. Moreover, unfortunately, a great deal of the new empirical work deals with trivial problems and arrives at only trivial conclusions, employing to this end unnecessarily sophisticated techniques of analysis to manipulate data that are suspect from the outset. The gloss of science may lend a temporary, fake respectability to thoroughly bad or trivial findings, but investigators who blindly apply advanced statistical techniques to poorly formulated concepts and imperfect data are inviting disaster. Only when they are used with restraint and on appropriate data are the scientific, empirical

[17] Dahrendorf, *ibid.*, p. ix.
[18] Lance Davis, "Professor Fogel and the New Economic History," *The Economic History Review,* **29** (December 1966), 657.

methods that are gaining ground everywhere in the social sciences and in history worth having.

The progress of a science is measured in two ways: by its ability to explain more in terms of less, and by its power to generate testable hypotheses and theory. The first is summed up by the principle of parsimony, which should be applied nowhere more rigorously than in comparative education. The aim of the investigator who seeks to explain a particular phenomenon should not be to incorporate into his analysis as many factors, countries, and time periods as possible. Rather, by careful statement of hypotheses and insightful choice of concepts and cases, he should employ only as many variables and as many data as absolutely necessary to achieve satisfactory explanation. In other words, it is wrong for the comparative educator to act as if his primary responsibility were to immerse himself in the details of the educational systems of the world, squirreling away data, ready to use the maximum of information on every possible occasion to explain or prove some point or other. This is an inelegant and wholly pedantic approach to comparative education; properly done, the empirical method offers not the least, but the most, economical way to explain phenomena.

The second test of the empirical method is its heuristic potential. This is found not so much in the specific conclusions achieved with its aid, but in the process of investigation it mandates. As J. Bronowski has put it, "For this is the lesson of science, that the concept is more profound that its laws and the act of judging more critical than the judgment."[19]

[19] J. Bronowski, *Science and Human Values.* New York: J. Messner, 1956, p. 94.

10

Scientific Method and Comparative Education

Comparative Education as a Field of Inquiry

> *"It seems very pretty," she said when she had finished it, "but it's rather hard to understand!" (You see she didn't like to confess, even to herself, that she couldn't make it out at all.) "Somehow it seems to fill my head with ideas —only I don't exactly know what they are!"*

So far, this section has been concerned with the value of the method of science as a way of knowing and its major features as a way of investigating social reality. It is now necessary to consider the special characteristics of comparative education and the case for applying empirical methods to its study.

Comparative education began with observations about foreign peoples and their education and developed into descriptions of foreign school systems. Inherent in this work was the practical aim of borrowing from abroad useful educational devices for the improvement of education at home. The descriptive phase gradually expanded to include examination of the social, political, and historical context in which school systems developed. A further dimension was added to the description of these relationships as comparative educators proceeded to consider the dynamic interaction between education and its societal setting. Most recently, comparative education has entered yet a new phase in which cross-national data are used to test propositions about the relationship of education to society.

Comparative education is thus part of the wider attempt to explain phenomena, first, within educational systems and institutions, and second, surrounding education and linking it with its social environment. Attempts to do the first lead to a concern with the technology of education: the methods, practices, and outcomes of different modes of instruction, organization, supervision, administration, and finance. Where attention is paid to the teaching-learning process in a number of countries, educational psychology and particularly psychometrics are especially relevant. Insofar as comparative education is concerned with pedagogy, the work has largely been done by teachers, administrators, and educational psychologists seeking to comprehend and possibly to improve the instructional work of the schools, and it is useful to term this branch of the subject comparative pedagogy. But to the extent that comparative education has looked outside the confines of the classroom and the school system, its concerns and its data have overlapped with the interests of social scientists, some of whom have recently undertaken systematic comparative study of education as a social phenomenon.

Comparative education has one foot firmly planted in pedagogy and the other in the wider area of the social sciences. Concern with the form and function of the school has, however, united these two aspects of the field by concentrating attention on similar kinds of data and complementary topics. A second unifying element, and possibly a more important one, has recently become apparent in a common movement toward empirical and quantitative methods of inquiry. Notably, the IEA study described in Chapter 6 has welded together the two aspects of comparative education: concern with technology of education (comparative pedagogy) and with the interaction of schooling and its social context.[1] Comparative education in its most recent phase emerges as the attempt to use cross-national data to test propositions about the relationship between education and society and between teaching practices and learning outcomes.

Characteristic Problems of Comparative Education

> *"Well, in* our *country," said Alice, still panting a little, "you'd generally get to somewhere else—if you ran very fast for a long time as we've been doing."*
>
> *"A slow sort of country!" said the Queen. "Now,* here, *you see, it takes all the running* you *can do, to keep in the same place."*

The serious problems of the field are not hard to perceive. For the comparative educator the nagging questions persist: why do we know so little for certain in comparative education, and why does comparative education hardly figure at all in the list of recognized fields of comparative study (history, sociology, religion, literature, economics, political science)? A recent compendium of scientific findings about human behavior includes a great deal of material on education, but can report nothing that relies on cross-national research in this area.[2] Similarly, a review article by an outstandingly well-informed scholar on the status of comparative studies in the United States makes not a single mention of comparative education.[3] A number of problems appear fundamental to comparative education and presumably must be met head on and overcome if

[1] Torsten Husén (ed.), *International Study of Achievement in Mathematics: A Comparison of Twelve Countries.* New York: John Wiley, 1967.

[2] Bernard Berelson and Gary A. Steiner, *Human Behavior: An Inventory of Scientific Findings.* New York: Harcourt, Brace, and World, Inc., 1964.

[3] Edward Shils, "Seeing It Whole," *The Times Literary Supplement,* July 28, 1966, pp. 647–648.

the field is ever to realize its potential. They are the problems of bias, utility of results, and eclecticism in both methodology and data.

Bias may arise at every stage of the comparative educator's work, from the identification of problems to the collection of data, their interpretation, and the conclusions drawn from them. Ethnocentrism is an obvious source of bias in comparative education: inevitably investigators view foreign societies through a selective and distorting screen interposed by their cultural experience.[4] But there is a vastly more important source of bias embedded in the whole field of comparative education and, indeed, in the social sciences in general. This entire edifice of knowledge is part of the intellectual achievement of the Western world during the past two centuries and reflects the secularism, liberalism, and humanism of the modern Western tradition. Just as the development of the physical sciences in the West has been the story of man's attempt to extend his control over his physical environment, so the development of the social sciences similarly has sought to extend man's control over his social environment. Difficult though it may be for the observer brought up in this tradition to recognize, the instrumental view itself provides a value system that must bias perceptions. For example, movement toward a secular, humanistic, liberal, and industrialized society is equated with progress and is endowed with positive value. Comparative educators have fully shared this bias, as their writings reveal. Until very recently their attention was concentrated almost exclusively on Western-type societies and their consideration of other societies is still too frequently cast in terms of movement toward Western structures and processes. The tendency has been to regard non-Western nations as in some way primitive forms and to assume that their natural development will follow Western precedents. Moreover, these attitudes have not been a monopoly of comparative educators and social scientists in the West; they have been shared in good measure by their colleagues in Japan, India, and a host of contemporary developing countries.

As a result, comparative education has devoted primary attention

[4] See, G. Z. F. Bereday, "The Significance of Cultural Bias: The United States and England," *Comparative Method in Education*. New York: Holt, Rinehart and Winston, 1964.

to problems of change and progress: relating education to economic growth, social amelioration, and political development. Compared to the volumes produced on these topics, the amount of attention paid to conservation of existing institutions has been insignificant. Moreover, those who have concerned themselves with the maintenance and continuity of present social and cultural modes have been labelled traditionalist and reactionary. Yet there are clearly some very important and legitimate problems to be examined in this area.

The culturally imposed filter affects not only the problems selected for study, but also the data. It is merely trite to observe that the selection of some problems and the ignoring of others will inevitably condition the type of data collected. But the problem is compounded in comparative education, where an investigator from an alien culture often is unable to recognize the relevance of certain types of data for the solution of the problem he has chosen. When the comparative educator examines the relationship between education and economic development in, say, India, he is naturally attracted to an examination of those formal educational institutions for which statistics and data have been collected. Among these data he tends to search out just those elements he has learned are important in the models with which he is familiar. What has not already been identified for him and what has not in his past experience seemed to have much importance may not be taken into account. Thus, modernization and education in India may be examined on the basis of the number of technical school places opened and filled. This procedure simply reflects the role of formal technical education in Western societies. Yet the most important means of modernization in Indian society may be increasing availability of automobiles, bicycles, water pumps, and so forth—all the Western-type machines that impose on their operators disciplines of use, maintenance, and repair. Insofar as the comparative educator is interested in examining the relationship between education and development, he would be utterly misled by giving attention just to the formal system of education and neglecting the informal educational effects of introducing Western machinery.

One stimulus to improved work in a field is the ease of movement between the research findings in the field and their practical applications. Although comparative interest sprang from a desire to improve education by studying foreign models, the difficulties involved in extensive foreign borrowing eventually became apparent. The later comparative studies of the role of education in society provided a mass of descriptive and sometimes interpretive writing that provided little practical guidance to educational policy makers, whatever may have been its value for scholarship. One of the major incentives for a reawakened interest in comparative education in recent years had been the expectation that lessons drawn from comparative study could be used to aid in the development of the new nations. However, comparative education still remains far from realizing these hopes and the findings of comparative educators as yet rarely enter into the considerations of planners of national education systems, for their predictive value has yet to be demonstrated.

Another important problem of comparative education warrants discussion. Is it possible to distinguish clearly a problem in comparative education from problems in the economics of education, sociology of education, and so on? In other words, is there a clear definition of comparative education as a field of inquiry? If at present comparative education is suffering from an identity crisis, one reason may be its eclecticism. When anthropologists, sociologists, economists, political scientists, historians, and philosophers can all make some claim to expertise in the field, it becomes extremely difficult to identify its limits with respect to both method and data. There is no consensus about the area of discourse over which comparative educators properly may range.

The ranking of a new field of inquiry in the "pecking order" of academic respectability depends on the "hardness" of its data or the rigor of its methods. As an eminent economist expressed the idea,

. . . economics is by its nature a softer and less exact science than, say, conventional physics. Now in a hard, exact science a practitioner does not really have to know much about methodology. Indeed, even if he is definitely a misguided methodologist, the subject itself has a self-cleansing property which renders harmless his aberrations. By contrast, a scholar in economics who is fundamentally confused concerning the relationship of definition, tautology, logical implication, empirical hypothesis, and factual refutation may spend a lifetime shadow-boxing with reality. In a sense, therefore, in order to earn his daily bread as a fruitful contributor to knowledge, the practitioner of an intermediately hard science like economics must come to terms with methodological problems. I stress the importance of intermediate hardness because when one descends lower still, say to certain areas of sociology that are almost completely without substantive content, it may not matter much one way or the other what truths or errors about scientific method are involved—for the reason that nothing matters.[5]

The data used in comparative education are notoriously "soft," and consequently there is a high premium on methodological rigor. Yet comparative education cannot be regarded as an enterprise with its own *raison d'être* so long as it has neither a well substantiated theoretical framework nor distinctive concepts of its own. Comparative education can expect no assured place in the hierarchy of academic studies until its data and methods are clarified and their relation to one another recognized.

The Potential of Comparative Education

> *"If there's no meaning in it," said the King, "that saves a world of trouble, you know, as we needn't try to find any."*

These multifarious difficulties nothwithstanding, the field undoubtedly contains considerable potential, arising from two sources: the special value of the cross-national dimension for studying educational issues and the arena for interdisciplinary collaboration that the field provides.

Not all propositions in education and society require cross-national treatment, but with respect to two types of validation, cross-national work is mandatory. First, quite obviously, some

---

[5] Paul Anthony Samuelson, *Foundations of Economic Analysis.* New York: Atheneum, 1965, p. ix.

generalizations simply cannot be tested by using data from one country alone since there is not sufficient variation in the single case. For example, a test of the hypothesis that there is a relation between centralization of national educational administration and students' achievement levels inevitably requires cross-national inquiry. Second, the single case permits no more than a particular statement to be made, and it is only on the basis of cross-national research that propositions established by study of a single case can be generalized and further refined. This point merits further discussion.

Even in single-country studies, the cross-national dimension can enrich explanation. Confined to domestic data, a historical study of the expansion of higher education in the United States may be able to provide genetic explanations for its present state, but there is no doubt that such a particular study will gain by being set in the context of higher educational developments in other countries. Of course the expansion of higher education in the United States cannot be properly understood apart from such foreign development as the flight of German intellectuals after the failure of the 1848 Revolution in Prussia, the foreign experiences of American students and professors, and the emphasis on graduate research imported from Germany. Here is the classic justification for the comparative dimension: including foreign data in a single-country study enhances explanation of domestic phenomena. But, more important, if a hypothesis is tested within the confines of only one society, there can be no certainty that the conclusions do not have merely parochial validity. Suppose that a study of the social outcomes of the expansion of higher education in the United States shows that expansion has promoted intergenerational social mobility from lower to middle socioeconomic levels, but not from middle to upper levels. Even if this result is regarded as having a high level of accuracy for the United States, it is only by investigating the same topic in other countries that the full value of the United States finding can be exploited. Suppose that in extending this study to England, similar conclusions are reached. A double bonus is derived from the broadened scope of the study: the United States findings are further validated, and the statement about the relationship between the expansion of higher education and social mobility in the United States now becomes more general.

Alternatively, it may be revealed that what was found to be true of the relationship between higher education and social mobility in the United States is not true in England. This should lead immediately to the suspicion that the relationship is much more complex than first thought. When confronted with evidence of two different sets of social outcomes as a result of similar educational expansion in the two countries, the investigator is forced to abandon any simplistic explanation of the phenomena. He must reconsider the entire problem and undertake an investigation embracing more factors and more cases in order to develop a more comprehensive theory. One of the great advantages of comparative investigation is precisely this heuristic potential.

Comparative education can provide an arena where representatives of different disciplines come together to their mutual benefit, forcing investigators out of their narrow specializations.[6] The field has often been considered a natural candidate for interdisciplinary work by reason of the particular problems and data it treats. Indeed, many of the important topics that fall to comparative education can be handled satisfactorily only in an interdisciplinary manner. For example, no study of education and national development is conceivable solely within the confines of a single discipline; it must draw from a wide range of behavioral and social sciences. However, comparative education is multi- rather than interdisciplinary in both its origins and current state. Every branch of social science has made use of educational data from various countries; in return, comparative education has drawn data and concepts from the social sciences. As previously stressed, this has been a cause of much confusion concerning the scope and limits of the field. But its multidisciplinary character could be transformed into an interdisciplinary effort if the data, concepts, and methods of the several social

[6] This is not to suggest, of course, that an amateur in, say, economics is bound to be better than a professional in the investigation of a problem in comparative education which has an economic dimension, but the very lack of a vested interest in the orthodox methods of a particular field may be a stimulus to fresh and fruitful approaches. See David C. McClelland, *The Achieving Society*. Princeton, N.J.: Van Nostrand, 1961, pp. vii–xi.

sciences were systematically focused on the testing of specific socio-educational propositions. Then, what has been a constant source of difficulty might become instead an asset.

There are many topics of common interest to educational investigators and social scientists. All may share an interest in the social dimensions of education. For example, its political ramifications will interest political scientists, as much as educators. Because all aspects of the society cannot be treated together at one time, problems in comparative education cannot profitably be expressed holistically in terms of relationships between education as a whole and society as a whole. Rather, they must be expressed in terms of some specific aspect of education and some limited sector of the total societal context. Therefore it is necessary to consider the total social context as made up of several overlapping sectors: for example, the economy, the ideology (religious, political, and social), the social structure, and the political structure. Consequently, among the common problems comparative education is concerned with are the schools and economic development, the impact of different ideologies on education, education and class structure, and education and the formation of social and political elites. These categories are not entirely arbitrary, but coincide with some major approaches to the study of society, as represented by the several social sciences. At the same time it should be emphasized that they are by no means the only ways of categorizing the total area of interest in comparative education.

Because so many propositions can profitably be tested cross-nationally, it should not be surprising that the area of comparative education is occupied by educators and social scientists equally. Yet comparative education is potentially more than a congeries of data and perspectives from the social sciences applied to education in different countries. Neither the topic of education nor the cross-national dimension is central to any of the social sciences; nor are social science concerns and the cross-national dimension central to the work of educators. The field of comparative education is best defined as an intersection of the social sciences, education, and cross-national study. Consequently, a problem in comparative education is the common concern of both social scientists and educators, but the exclusive concern of neither.

There are, of course, severe problems involved in interdisciplinary studies. Commonly they have been accused of sacrificing depth and rigorousness to breadth and modishness. In addition, specialists in one discipline have difficulty in understanding the concepts, assumptions, and modes of proof of other disciplines. They often find it very difficult to appreciate the strategies, let alone the tactics, employed by other specialists to tackle a problem. But apart from the common focus of study (explanation of specific educational phenomena in their social context), there is one fundamental factor that promises to promote depth and rigorousness while uniting the disciplines engaged in comparative education. This is the scientific method, a mode of inquiry that is not merely a set of procedures or techniques, but an approach toward establishing belief.

Everything that has been presented in this section has pointed to the indispensable role of comparative work in social science explanation of educational phenomena. The implication that must be drawn from this is that comparative education is not just an exotic excursion from the main track of education studies, but that the comparative method provides one of the major routes for validating the most important propositions about education and society. Where controlled experimentation is impossible, controlled investigation, which inevitably calls for comparative study, is essential.

It is certainly important to identify more precisely than ever the substantive problems of education and society that demand attention and that can provide the arena for fruitful contributions from the social sciences. Moreover, not only is comparative study required for satisfactory explanation in problems of education and society, but the empirical methods of the social sciences must be embraced if the full potential of the comparative approach is to be realized. Of central importance then, will be the effort to develop in comparative education a systematic, controlled, empirical, and critical methodology. We now turn to a discussion of that practical task.

Part Three

THE METHOD
OF SCIENCE IN
COMPARATIVE EDUCATION

"Why," said the Dodo, "the best way to explain it is to do it."

11

Introduction:
Identifying the Problem

> *. . . the Mock Turtle drew a long breath, and said "That's very curious!"*
>
> *"It's all about as curious as it can be," said the Gryphon.*

Part One analyzed the modes of inquiry that have characterized comparative education up to the present. Part Two concentrated on the main features of the scientific approach, with special reference to problems in the social sciences in general and comparative education in particular. The task remaining is to show how scientific method can be employed systematically in comparative education. This part is concerned above all with practical considerations. It will discuss how to select a problem, how to construct a hypothesis within the framework of a theory, and how to handle concepts and operationalize them by the choice of indicators. It will further consider the sampling of countries, the collection and manipulation of data, and the interpretation of results. These procedures are the implementation in practice of the scientific strategy.

Scientific questions arise when we already know enough about a subject to ask the question "how?" At this stage, information about a particular set of phenomena has engendered some thoughts (more or less definite) about the way the phenomena are related. These ideas will have been drawn variously from observation, from study of accepted authorities, from intuitive notions about the way the real world works, and from what the conventional wisdom suggests. For example, a problem in comparative education might arise as follows. From personal experience and reading one acquires information and insights regarding the educational system of one's own country. Then, knowledge about the educational system of another country is accumulated either from firsthand experience or from secondary sources. At this point similarities and differences often become obvious and lead to a search for explanations. Contrasts abound: American children in public school do not receive formal religious instruction, whereas English children in state-provided schools do. In European school systems, a relatively small proportion of the seventeen- to eighteen-year-old children are in school; in the United States the proportion is very large. Sometimes it is the similarities rather than the differences that strike home. The basic units of school systems, the classrooms, are remarkably alike all over the world: teachers sit at the front of the room, students sit behind desks; a familiar tension connects the two; information generally flows from the former to the latter; textbooks, notebooks, and blackboards are ubiquitous. Or, on a more abstract level, the observer may note that the direction of educational reform over the last twenty years has been similar in a number of European countries. Curiosity about such similarities or differences will inevitably raise the questions "why?" and "how?" In this way the demand for explanation arises.

Explanation derives from many sources. One investigator, in trying to explain the difference in religious content in English and American public school curricula, may be satisfied to observe that religion is more generally influential in English life than it is in the United States. Another may explain the similarities among the European countries in the trends of educational reform by alluding to his firm belief in the inevitability of progress. Or, noting that some European countries are relatively slow in introducing educational reforms and others relatively advanced, he may be content with an explanation based on certain historians' views of the "progressive nature of Protestantism" and the "conservative ideology of Catholicism." All these are examples of the use of conventional wisdom, established authority, or a priori thinking and intuition. This early stage of browsing among the data and the authorities, of speculation and deduction, is extremely valuable. Interest leads to hunches, hunches to tentative statements, and a highly creative part of the total process of problem solving takes place. Through a series of intellectual leaps the investigator develops a set of questions, presumed relationships, and cause-and-effect statements necessarily preliminary to scientific investigation.

Investigation proper begins only when the researcher transfers his main attention from the countries, their educational systems, and the intriguing differences and similarities among them to the problem he wishes to solve.[1] The first stage of inquiry into educational systems is dominated by the desire to amass data and simply to know more "facts." Once the problem is generated, however, more facts are very often of no further help. The investigator's most urgent need is a criterion to help him distinguish the relevant from the irrelevant. This change of focus from preoccupation with the variety of data to preoccupation with devising methods to help solve the problem is crucial. The obvious analogy is the distinction between a big-game hunter and a zoologist. The former shoots whatever prey takes his fancy or happens to pass across his gun-sights. He hunts for the exotic and arranges his trophies in arbitrary categories. By contrast, the zoologist collects specimens in a disciplined manner. His purpose is to illustrate special phenomena and to help explain problems in his field.

Thus, paradoxical though it may seem, an important stage in comparative education begins when concentration on the variety of educational systems ends and attention is turned toward solving a problem. Indeed our central contention is that browsing among

[1] Brian Holmes, *Problems in Education: A Comparative Approach.* London: Routledge and Kegan Paul, 1965, chap. 4.

the data, accumulating more information, and arranging it in various ways can have value only as a preliminary to investigation. If collection is considered an end in itself, comparative education becomes no more than big-game hunting, antiquarianism, or even voyeurism. Not only is the potential of a comparative investigation wasted by stopping short after merely the preliminaries have been completed, but too much attention may be devoted to them, so that neither time nor energy is available for the next stages of the enterprise.

12

Two Model Hypotheses

"What is the use of repeating all that stuff?" the Mock
Turtle interrupted, "if you don't explain it as you go on?
It's by far the most confusing thing that I ever heard!"

In Part Two the general principles and strategy of scientific research
were described with some examples. In order to illustrate the necessary steps in performing an actual investigation, two topics in
comparative education will now be discussed as sources of model
working hypotheses. Each step in investigation will be illustrated
by reference to these two model hypotheses chosen for the assistance they can give in illustrating the practice of empirical investigation. Each topic has been selected to represent a different set of
problems: one is in an area already well studied, and is consequently easier to handle. The other has been deliberately selected
from a much less frequently visited domain, where concepts and

data are more diffuse, and where the topic is far less amenable to empirical, quantified treatment.[1]

The first problem-topic derives from a theory of the relationship between schools and the economy. There is some evidence that the wealth of a nation and the development of its school system go hand in hand, perhaps even depend on one another, though it is uncertain which is cause and which effect. Certainly, economic growth arises from the accumulation of knowledge and capital. Although the most productive investments are evidently those that open rich, easily accessible stores of natural resources (such as, fertile land, oil, coal, and ores), the concept of capital and capital formation should not be restricted to buildings, machines, coal mines, and so forth. Investment in the health, education, and training of the population also appears to be vital to the long-term growth of the economy.

Considerable work has already been done in this field, concepts have been refined, data amassed, and some quite specific relationships formulated. For example, Friedrich Edding has shown that educational expansion is generally limited by a country's ability to increase its output of wealth.[2] Moreover, periods of sustained economic growth generally appear to be preceded by certain minimum levels of primary school enrollment.[3] Several stages of economic growth and concomitant stages of literacy among the population have been roughly distinguished, and research suggests that the importance of literacy rates for economic growth is not constant, but varies according to the particular stage of growth attained.[4] Portions of a theory on the relationship between the schools and the economy have been relatively well developed through empirical investigation.

---

[1] Of course there are many other important areas of interest open to comparative study, besides the two selected for demonstration purposes. See Appendix B for a sample list of topics in the form of tentative hypotheses.

[2] F. Edding, *Internationale Tendenzen in der Entwicklung der Ausgaben für Schulen und Hochschulen.* Kiel: Institut für Weltwirtschaft an der Universität Kiel, 1958; and see Chap. 6.

[3] Alexander L. Peaslee, "Primary School Enrollments and Economic Growth," *Comparative Education Review,* 11 (February 1967), 57–67, and see Chap. 6.

[4] Mary Jean Bowman and C. Arnold Anderson, "Concerning the Role of Education in Development" in Clifford Geertz (ed.), *Old Societies and New States.* New York: The Free Press, 1963, and see Chap. 6.

From the tentative theory about the relationship between the economy and the schools, the following hypothesis is proposed as a demonstration model.

1. *Countries where the level of educational development is high relative to the level of economic development will experience rapid economic growth subsequently; countries where the educational level is low relative to the economic level will experience slower rates of economic growth subsequently.*[5]

The hypothesis asserts first that higher levels of educational growth prime the pump of economic development. It further asserts that a high educational level performs this function if, and only if, it is high enough to stay ahead of rising economic levels. Whereas the hypothesis stems from the theory relating the economy and the schools, it focuses on one specific element of that theory. It asserts a relationship, states the order of that relationship, and specifies general conditions under which the relationship is held to operate. Clearly one task of any theory seeking to explain the relationship between the schools and the economy will be to show how the level of schooling affects subsequent economic growth. This is precisely what the hypothesis invites us to examine. But it does not invite us to examine many other important segments of a general theory of the relationship between the economy and the schools, such as the effect of the level of economic growth on the expansion of education. For this a complementary study based on another hypothesis would be needed. Though the hypothesis represents an important part of the general theory from which it springs, it by no means represents the entire theory. Moreover, the hypothesis is neither descriptive nor parochial nor trivial. It is a statement about a relationship under certain general conditions; it is not a particular statement about the experience of any particular country. Thus it asserts a general rule.

The second model hypothesis for illustrating the application of

[5] This hypothesis is adapted from a study by the U.N. Research Institute for Social Development. See Nancy Baster with Muthu Subramanian, *Aspects of Social and Economic Growth: A Pilot Statistical Study.* Report no. 1. Geneva: UNRISD, 1965.

empirical methods is drawn from a much more tentative theory about ideology and education.

The rationale (justification) for the hypothesis is that there may be a relation between schools and the religious contexts in which they operate. Differences in curricula, teaching methods, and the structure of educational systems seem to go hand in hand with differences in religious ideology.[6] Though some work has been done on these phenomena and many data have been collected, understanding of the relationships involved is very limited and imprecise. Ideally, one would like to know about not only the existence and direction of relationships between schools and religious ideology, but also about the degree of influence one has on the other under specified circumstances. More specifically, it would be valuable to understand the relationships between curriculum, school procedures, enrollment ratios, and so on, and different religious ideologies. Is Catholicism associated with inadequate provision of elementary education, as some have asserted? Are there any connections between modes of discipline in the schools and different denominational outlooks? Is the spread of secondary education inimical to transcendental belief? No doubt most observers could venture answers to these questions and even produce some supporting data, but scientific or empirical substantiation is absent. In investigating a problem of this kind, theory is vague, concepts are poorly defined, relationships are obscure, and objective data sadly lacking.

The second model hypothesis, formulated for the purposes of demonstration, is,

2. *The more otherworldly the religious beliefs, the greater the emphasis on theoretical studies in education; the less otherwordly the religious beliefs, the greater the emphasis on practical studies.*

This hypothesis asserts that there is a relationship between emphasis on studies that have no immediate application to this world

---

[6] P. E. Levasseur, *La statistique de l'enseignement primaire.* Rome: Imprimerie Nationale de J. Bertero, 1892. See also Chap. 5, and N. Hans,

and a religious value system stressing the importance of a future life. Note that this hypothesis, too, does not assert a causal relationship; the state of the theory does not permit it. At this point the best that can be done is to assert the existence of covariation between otherworldliness and a particular curricular emphasis. Not only is the theory less definite than in the previous example, but the concepts in which the hypothesis is expressed are much more vague. This is so partly because the concepts are inherently more difficult to define, partly because they are highly subjective, and partly because much less work has been done to validate them as useful categories in empirical research. Though it yet remains to be shown that the concept "otherworldliness" has a useful empirical content, the hypothesis expresses a relationship between the two variables and is therefore more than merely descriptive; and it asserts the existence of a general rule and therefore is not parochial.

This hypothesis may be considered part of a larger attempt to investigate how a set of societal values is related to education. If the hypothesis is confirmed, part of the theoretical structure from which it came will be strengthened. Establishing the proposition that religious values embodied in teachers, students, and the rest of society are associated with a specific pattern of studies will encourage the testing of similar hypotheses asserting a relationship between curricular emphases and other ideological variables (for example, democratic outlooks, egalitarian beliefs, or specific sectarian creeds). Hence, this hypothesis is not trivial, if only because it has heuristic potential.

Each hypothesis is drawn from a different theory, employs different concepts, and is at a different level of specificity. Nevertheless they have several important features in common. Each is a statement about two variables; each states a relationship between them. In both instances the variables are stated in terms broad enough to permit generalization, but specifically enough to permit quantification. The term educational level in the first hypothesis is preferred to the terms primary school enrollment ratio or cultural level because the first would be too specific and the second too

Comparative Education: A Study of Educational Factors and Traditions. London: Routledge and Kegan Paul, 1949, pp. 85–105.

general. Similarly, both hypotheses not only state that a relationship exists between the variables, but specify that relationship as far as possible. For example, the first hypothesis predicts that a relatively higher educational level will be associated with economic growth at a later date and that the association will be positive. These conditions for a good hypothesis establish important rules of the game: they contain the implications for empirical measurement and testing as well as the criteria for confirmation or disconfirmation of the hypothesis.

The kinds of hypotheses that can be formulated depend on the state and nature of the theory surrounding the problem to be investigated. In the first topic (the relation between schools and the economy) because of the greater precision of concepts and the already established results of prior empirical investigation, relatively precise and refined hypotheses can be formulated. In the second topic (the relation between religious outlook and schooling) because of the extremely vague nature of concepts and the absence of "hard" data, only the most general and tentative hypotheses may be feasible. In neither case can causality be posited, for theory and data are insufficient, and extraneous factors probably affect both variables in each hypothesis in as yet indeterminate ways.

13

Concepts and Indicators

> "When I use a word," Humpty Dumpty said, in rather a scornful tone, "it means just what I choose it to mean—neither more nor less."
>
> "The question is," said Alice, "whether you can make words mean so many different things."
>
> "The question is," said Humpty Dumpty, "which is to be Master—that's all."

A hypothesis is a statement about a relationship between two or more variables. Each variable is specified in terms of concepts, which are man-made categories imposed upon the phenomena. For example "economic level" is a concept imposed upon phenomena observed in the real world, and it becomes a variable when related in a hypothesis to another concept, such as "educational level." Similarly, in the second model hypothesis, the concept "otherworldliness" becomes a variable when it is related to the concepts "theoretical studies" and "practical studies."

The first step in the empirical measurement of concepts is to operationalize them. This requires defining the concept on the basis of the various measures of it that can be made.

Model Hypothesis 1

In the first hypothesis it follows that a beginning to operationalizing the concept "educational level" is made by considering how it might be measured. There are many possibilities. From statistics already gathered in most countries, the proportion of each relevant age group enrolled in formal instruction (enrollment ratios) from primary through higher education may be measured. Another way of measuring educational level might be in financial terms: expenditure on education as a fraction of gross national product. A third measure might be derived from the fraction of the total labor force employed in education or from the average pupil-teacher ratio for the whole country. These measures are all separate indicators of educational level and have been widely used in research.

There is convenience in using these indicators already available in the published sources, but they share one disadvantage. They fail to encompass one entire dimension of the concept of educational level, for they refer only to the input aspects of the educational system and omit all the output aspects. Although they measure the money, buildings, teacher time, student time, and so on, put into the schools, they do not measure levels of achievement, a major output of the schools. An operational definition of the concept is presumably not complete without indicators of the educational achievement of the school population, in part or in its entirety, and of the adult population. Literacy rates are often used for this purpose, because internationally comparable measures of pupil achievement are much more difficult and expensive to obtain. Where even literacy rates are not available, or where the statistics are suspect, the investigator may be forced to use such indicators as newspaper circulation per head of the population or library book circulation per head or even a count of the number of bridegrooms who sign the marriage register with their names rather than making a cross.[1]

When operationalizing the concept of economic level, there are also many indicators to choose from: gross national product per capita, energy production per capita, and industrial production per man-hour are commonly employed. Data for these indicators, too, are readily available for many countries. The third concept, economic growth, is based on a comparison of levels of gross national product, or national income, at the beginning and at the end of a given time period. From these figures, average annual rates of growth can be derived.

Compared to the difficulties raised by the second model hypothesis, the educational and economic concepts and indicators here are all relatively straightforward and measurable. However, the investigator should always be aware of the imperfections inevitably built into his indicators. The concept of economic level, for example, has inherent logical and statistical difficulties that the unwary investigator might not suspect.[2] There are inevitable shortcomings in many national statistical series of GNP figures. GNP is itself an aggregate of a host of separate totals of production from the different sectors and industries of the economy. In order to be able to aggregate automobiles and wheat, for example, both must be reduced to a common denominator—money value. However, some serious statistical problems then must be faced. Moreover, errors are likely in the separate estimates of the value of output in the different sectors and industries and therefore the aggregate GNP figure reported in the national statistical handbook may be even more likely to contain errors.

If there are serious difficulties in measuring a nation's GNP, international comparisons a fortiori are still more questionable. Different countries may use different statistical conventions in arriving at aggregate figures, to say nothing of the variations be-

---

[1] Statistics on literacy in England in the eighteenth and early nineteenth centuries have been collected on this basis. See R. K. Webb, *The British Working Class Reader, 1790–1848*. London: George Allen and Unwin, 1955, p. 21, for criticism of this method.

[2] See Oskar Morgenstern, *On the Accuracy of Economic Observations,* second edition. Princeton, N.J.: Princeton University Press, 1965. Especially chapters XIV and XV.

tween national statistical services in efficiency and accuracy when collecting and manipulating the raw data. Economists accept GNP figures as the best available measure of economic level, but in full awareness that the figures are only estimates and tend to understate severely the incomes of less-developed countries.

Model Hypothesis 2

The second hypothesis advances a highly abstract concept—otherworldliness. To operationalize it, the investigator has to exercise a great deal more creativity and imagination than in measuring a widely used and workaday concept such as economic level. Otherworldliness is more abstract in the sense that it is further removed from direct implications for measurement. But an imaginative consideration of the dimensions of the concept may point toward the indicators by which the concept may be identified.

At least three important dimensions may be distinguished as part of the concept of otherworldliness: the eschatological, the organizational, and the ritualistic. Eschatology refers to the elements in the religion that recognize the existence and nature of life after death. The second dimension, organization, is concerned with the worldly structure, sometimes the bureaucracy, through which the religion operates. Ritual, the third dimension, incorporates the symbols and behavior through which the religion is expressed. Though other meanings of the concept undoubtedly exist, these three will suffice to illustrate the process of operationalizing a highly abstract concept.

Now that some dimensions of the concept have been identified, indicators must be chosen to measure them. Though it is not easy to deal quantitatively with such a doctrine as life after death, the very least that can be done is to establish for each system of belief two simple categories: either life after death is a tenet of the ideology or it is not. But further precision is desirable and may perhaps be obtained by a scale representing different intensities of the doctrine of life after death. In some systems this doctrine may be central to the entire religious outlook. It may be formulated very explicitly, and rewards and punishments for behavior in this life may be seen as accruing primarily in a future life. If Hell, Heaven, Nirvana, Paradise, reincarnation, Judgment Day, and messianic beliefs figure prominently, the religion presumably would earn a place at the upper end of the scale; systems of belief where such considerations do not exist, are less explicitly stated, or are less central to the prescribed code of behavior would be assigned lower positions on the scale.

Indicators of the second dimension of otherworldliness, the organizational, may be found in the existence and importance in the religion of some kind of priesthood and the degree to which it is differentiated from the lay population (perhaps by reference to length of training or priestly vows of poverty, celibacy, and other marks of withdrawal from the mainstream of social life). Presumably the structure of church administration (if one exists) and the sources of religious authority provide additional indicators. Thus a church drawing its authority from a democratic assembly of laymen (Congregationalist) may be classed as less otherworldly than one that derives its supreme authority directly from Christ's Vicar on earth (Roman Catholic).

The third dimension of otherworldliness can be measured in terms of ritual. Is there a sacred language? Is knowledge of the sacred language spread widely or confined to a few? Are there mysteries relating to important elements of the religion? Do ceremonial behavior and the sacred quality of ritual objects figure prominently in religious practices? Like the indicators of eschatology, these questions demand more than mere binary (yes/no) answers. They call for estimates of the intensity of the presence of these elements.

Besides the stated concept of otherworldliness, another concept, religiosity, is implicit in the hypothesis. Because cross-national comparisons are called for, the ultimate purpose is not to rank religions, but to rank nations. Assuming that it is possible by use of appropriate indicators to rank religions along a scale of otherworldliness, the implied concept must be identified and operationalized before otherworldliness can be related to other variable, educational emphasis. The fact that a nation is characterized by a highly otherworldly religious tradition does not necessarily mean that its public policies are dominated by that religion. In essence, not only is a measure of the otherworldly quality of the dominant faith required, but also a measure of religiosity, that is, the extent of religious influence on the nation. It may be measured by the percentage of the population professing the dominant faith and from the degree of preference awarded to the state religion, if one exists. Preferences may be indicated by the presence of state-mandated religious holidays, denominational school instruction, restrictions on the practice of other religions, or civil disabilities imposed on religious nonconformists.

The remaining concept in the second model hypothesis refers to educational emphasis—theoretical versus practical. This too requires operationalizing. For the purposes of the hypothesis, theoretical studies may be defined as those that not only have a high level of abstraction, but that also are remote from direct application in business and industry. Practical studies refer to those fairly directly related to occupations in the business and industrial world. Because all studies have elements of the abstract and theoretical as well as practical and vocational implications, the choice of indicators for the two categories is not simple. As far as higher education is concerned, the pair of subjects, natural sciences versus engineering, may be proposed as an indicator of theoretical-practical emphasis. At the secondary level, participation in general academic schooling as compared with vocational training may be measured. Some obvious ways of quantifying each element of these pairs are: figures of student enrollments, number of graduates, and number of faculty. Ratios may then be calculated for each pair to serve as indicators of the emphasis, theoretical or practical, in the country's educational system.

The preceding discussion exemplifies the major problem facing the investigator when he selects indicators to operationalize his concepts. He is caught between the desire to encompass by his choice of indicators all the important dimensions of his concepts and the limitations imposed on him by the scarcity of time and resources. The particular concepts discussed can be operationalized in narrow or wide terms, depending on the number of indicators used and the extent to which they span the dimensions of the concept. But this discussion illustrates the normal dilemma of the investigator in the social sciences: he has to admit that his indicators could no doubt be improved upon, but he must hope that they do lend a precise, if limited, operational definition to his concepts.

14

Selecting the Cases

"... Let me see—how is it to be managed? I suppose
I ought to eat or drink something or other; but the great
question is 'What?' "

The great question certainly was "What?" Alice looked
all round her at the flowers and the blades of grass, but
she could not see anything that looked like the right
thing to eat or drink under the circumstances.

In order to test a comparative hypothesis, one has to select cases
for study. But the question immediately arises of how many cases
are enough. One is obviously inadequate. Two cases may be better
and have commonly been the basis for studies termed comparative,
but two-country studies also have their limitations.

For one thing they tend to highlight all differences between the two
countries chosen as possibly important in explaining the differences . . .,
even when some of those differences might turn out to be relatively
unimportant in comparisons involving a larger sample of countries.[1]

---

[1] David C. McClelland, "Motivational Patterns in Southeast Asia with
Special Reference to the Chinese Case," *The Journal of Social Issues,* **19**
(January 1963), 7.

A larger number of cases than two is often desirable for the satisfactory testing of a hypothesis. In general, the criteria for selection are threefold: the relevance of the cases to the hypothesis, control of the major extraneous variables, and economy of investigation.

Clearly, it is pointless to include in the sample countries to which the hypothesis cannot apply. Even where it does apply, if there are no data available, a country must be ruled out of the investigation. If a hypothesis deals with the impact of Christian denominational thought upon educational development, large portions of the world are automatically excluded. Conversely, priority for inclusion will generally go to those countries exemplifying to a marked degree the phenomena embraced by the hypothesis. For example, the first model hypothesis refers to rates of economic growth. Consequently, prime candidates for inclusion might be Japan, Austria, and the U. S. S. R., countries that have demonstrated high and sustained economic growth, and the United Kingdom, Ireland, and the United States, examples of countries with consistently low rates of economic growth.

Selection of cases also provides the opportunity to control the influence of gross extraneous factors. In the second hypothesis, where religious ideology is related to educational emphasis, at least two factors are obviously pertinent to the general topic, but are not the concern of this particular investigation. They are level of industrialization and level of educational development. It is preferable, therefore, to select countries with roughly similar levels, in order to limit their contaminating effects. However, the problem of controlling extraneous variables can rarely be solved simply by a judicious selection of countries. For example, the factors of other-worldliness and level of industrialization may be too entwined to be separated out simply by sampling; and while sampling may succeed in controlling for level of industrialization, it may be unable to control for other important variables, such as size of the population, political ideology, and the extent of foreign influence on the curriculum. Sampling alone cannot deal with the whole problem of interacting and intervening variables.[2]

---

[2] In these cases, statistical techniques such as factor analysis and regression analysis may be called for. See Fred N. Kerlinger, *Foundations of Behavioral*

Sampling, however, does have the great merit of focusing attention on those cases likely to help in testing the hypothesis. The central concern is always to prove or disprove the hypothesis in the most economical fashion, and the judicious selection of countries is a major way of achieving this. If too few countries are chosen, some degree of generality is sacrificed; but increasing the number of cases past a given point may not pay off significantly in greater generality and validity of results. Indeed, the consequence may be merely to confuse the investigation, render data collection unreliable and expensive, and complicate the analysis. The aim of scientific comparative education, after all, is not to amass as many data from as many countries as possible, but to explain as much as possible in the most economical manner.

Apart from these three general criteria for the selection of cases to study, four major types of samples may be distinguished: global, regional (multinational), regional (intranational), and cross-temporal.

In a global sample, selected data are gathered for all the countries of the world. Such comprehensive sampling is characteristic of studies ranking many countries according to specific criteria (for example, size of population, level of gross national product, rate of economic growth, degree of educational development, and so forth). An example of this type of comprehensive, or near-comprehensive, sampling is Harbison and Myers' study, *Education, Manpower and Economic Growth,* in which the authors categorize seventy-five countries in four levels of educational development.[3] The merit of such global collections of data is that they provide convenient sources of information and generate hypotheses for closer study. But these benefits are not free. Even though modern information storage and retrieval systems operate at ever-decreasing

---

Research. New York: Holt, Rinehart and Winston, 1965, chap. 36; and M. J. Moroney, *Facts from Figures,* third edition, revised, Baltimore, Md.: Penguin Books, 1956, chap. 16.

[3] Frederick Harbison and Charles A. Myers, *Education, Manpower, and Economic Growth.* New York: McGraw-Hill, 1964. See also, Arthur S. Banks and Robert B. Textor, *A Cross-Polity Survey.* Cambridge, Mass.: The M.I.T. Press, 1963; Bruce M. Russett, et al., *World Handbook of Political and Social Indicators.* New Haven: Yale University Press, 1964; and *World Survey of Education* (3 vols.); Paris: UNESCO, 1955–1961.

cost per unit of information, global data are acquired, recorded, and disseminated only at great expense. Moreover, since the total universe of data has a temporal as well as a spatial dimension, a truly universal collection requires information about all countries at all points of time. Thus, even the largest collection of social and educational data now extant is far from encompassing all the data of possible pertinence to comparative education. In practice, the investigator must be content with a sample from the total group of contemporary countries, selected according to the general criteria just discussed.

However, comparison need not be between total national units only, even though the term comparative education has generally become synonymous with cross-national study of education. But both logically and methodologically the rubric of comparative education should cover comparisons among other kinds of units, whether larger or smaller than nations. For certain purposes, subcontinents or regions transcending national boundaries may be compared. In the second hypothesis, for example, it may be appropriate to consider Latin America as a whole, rather than country by country, as representative of Catholic ideology, or Scandinavia as a whole, as representative of Protestantism, and to compare these two transnational regions. Similarly, the case for intranational comparisons is also a strong one under certain circumstances, for this procedure may offer the opportunity to hold constant the structure and culture of the nation-state, one of the most important variables in comparative work. Moreover, intranational comparisons highlight real and important regional variations within each country, which international comparisons, using aggregate national data tend to obscure.[4] A single indicator may signify completely different variables in different parts of the country and therefore have low validity as an indicator for the nation as a whole. For example, in a rural area otherworldliness may be correlated with conservatism, traditionalism, or backwardness; in urban areas, it may be an indicator of radical progressive opposition

[4] See Erik Allardt, "Implications of Within-Nation Variations and Regional Imbalances for Cross-National Research," in Merritt and Rokkan (eds.), *Comparing Nations: The Use of Quantitative Data in Cross-National Research.* New Haven: Yale University Press, 1966.

to an advanced industrial society. In the United States, after all, the otherworldliness of the Southern Baptists has somewhat different social and cultural correlates from the otherworldliness of the hippies in the Haight-Ashbury district of San Francisco.

Just as comparisons need not necessarily be confined to nation-units, they need not be limited to one point in time. Comparisons between different points of time within a particular country, or a combination of the cross-sectional and cross-temporal dimensions, may be undertaken. For example, in a study of the relationships between urbanization and the development of primary education, a comparison might be made between England in the early nine-teenth and in the twentieth century in order to establish what variations there were in the relationship at different stages of in-dustrialization. This is not a historical study in the conventional sense, but a cross-temporal study, concerned with testing a hy-pothesis through comparison over time. A study that related urbani-zation and primary school development in a number of countries and used data from decades · when their respective levels of industrialization were roughly equivalent would exemplify a com-bination of cross-temporal and cross-national comparison.

Model Hypothesis 1

Which countries are to be selected for the first investigation, in the light of these general criteria? Given plentiful resources of time and money, one might take all the countries of the world, though even this would not cover every case, present and past. Even with limited resources, a nonjudgment sample could still be obtained by selecting say, every fifth country from an alphabetized list of all countries in the world. This would be a method of random sampl-ing. But in the interests of economy and relevance and in the hope of directly attacking the central issues raised by a hypothesis, so-called judgment samples are often called for. Because the present hypothesis is concerned with economic growth rates and their relation to educational-economic levels, the criterion of relevance calls for selection of countries on the basis of at least one of these factors. Growth rates are often available from standard sources or can be calculated easily, whereas the index of educational-economic levels will have to be calculated after collection and examination of data on each of the indicators. Therefore, for the purposes of illustrating practical approaches to this investigation, growth rates provide an appropriate criterion for selecting countries.

The criterion of economy indicates that fewer than all the countries of the world for which the relevant educational and economic data are available should be selected. Yet the sample must be large enough to reduce the probability that the results merely reflect the special circumstances of each of a small group of countries; that is, the sample of countries must be large enough to reduce the chance that the results are being systematically contaminated by extraneous factors. In fact, two samples will be used for this investigation: a group of countries demonstrating to a marked degree high rates of economic growth, and another demonstrating low rates. One sample contains sixteen countries, and the other twenty-six. Although the hypothesis does not explicitly predict a relationship between mediocre growth performance and nondescript educational-economic levels, this is one of its clear implications, and a later stage of investigation might well use a third sample of countries exhibiting middle-range growth.[5] High-growth countries are defined as those with growth rates of GNP per capita, 1957/1958 to 1964/1965, of above 4.5 per cent per annum, calculated from standard statistical sources. Nineteen such countries were identified, of which three were later rejected for lack of the necessary educational data. Low-growth countries are defined as those with growth rates below 2.5 per cent per annum. There were twenty-seven such countries, of which one was rejected for lack of data.

[5] Since we know that the economic and social structures of rich countries (irrespective of their growth rates) are different from those of poor countries, an obvious and pertinent alternative for selecting the sample is to examine separately groups of rich, poor, and possibly middle-range countries for the connection between the two variables. See Appendix A for a specimen investigation.

Model Hypothesis 2

The second model hypothesis calls for measurement of the relationship between otherworldliness of religion and educational emphasis (whether theoretical or practical) and suggests several alternative ways of choosing the sample of countries. One possibility is to compare different church-related educational systems within the confines of a single country. This procedure may then be repeated for a second and third country. A second possibility involves identifying geographical regions, whether larger or smaller than nation-states, where one religion is preeminent and then comparing educational emphases among them. For example, within many nations large and discrete territories may differ according to their religions: West Germany, Holland, and Ireland each are divided into predominantly Catholic and predominantly Protestant areas; several Balkan countries are divided among various Christian denominations, Eastern and Western; and Canada is divided between Catholic Quebec and the rest of the country. Given that educational data are available separately for these units, either of these bases for sampling is practical. A third possibility, and the one used for demonstration purposes in the following discussion, is to search for nation-states dominated by a particular religion or denomination and to correlate the characteristics of the religion with the relevant data on education.

A sample of countries to satisfy the triple criteria of relevance, control, and economy requires first of all a selection representing a range of major religions and denominations: for example, Hinduism, Islam, Roman Catholicism, Buddhism, Presbyterianism, Lutheranism, Anglicanism, and Judaism. Second, even the most casual glance at the countries of the world reveals a high degree of correlation between dominant religious persuasion and level of economic development. Among the poorer countries, Buddhism, Hinduism, and Islam are dominant, while no Protestant countries are represented; and generally the Judaeo-Christian persuasions predominate among the wealthier nations. Hence, the criterion of control demands selection of countries at similar economic levels, lest results purporting to show a relationship between otherworldliness and educational emphasis be contaminated by the influence of the economic factor.

Regarding economy, two points can be made. The first concerns the accessibility of data as a guide to the selection of cases. Educational data are likely to be equally available for most countries of the world, whereas, as far as we are aware, no systematically comparable data on otherworldliness exist to guide the choice of countries. The second consideration raises the question of how many cases are enough for this investigation to be satisfactory. Because the concept of otherworldliness is novel as an object of empirical investigation, a great deal of groundwork has to be done to clarify the concept and operationalize it before the main work of testing the hypothesis can begin. And before the empirical value of the central concept itself has been established, there is little advantage in taking a large number of countries. On the other hand, the sample must not be so small that any results, even the most perfect, might be reasonably attributed to chance.

In view of all of these considerations, two small groups of countries will be used for this investigation: seven low-income countries, representing a range of major world religions, and seven high-income countries, representing a range of denominations in the Judaeo-Christian tradition. In the first group, the countries selected to represent major religions are: India (Hindus, over 80 per cent of the total population), Pakistan and Egypt (Muslims, over 85 per cent), Bolivia and Peru (Roman Catholics, 95 per cent), and Thailand and Burma (Buddhists, 92 per cent). These seven countries have in common low figures of GNP per capita, below 180 United States dollars per capita for 1957. The second group of countries represents the Judaeo-Christian traditions. They have much higher GNP levels per capita, ranging from $516 to $1,380 (1957). In each of these countries the dominant religion is professed by over 80 per cent of the population. The countries are France, Ireland, and Italy (Roman Catholic); Scotland (Presbyterian); Sweden (Lutheran); England (Anglican); and Israel (Jewish).

15

Collecting the Data

Of course the first thing to do was to make a grand survey of the country she was going to travel through. "It's something very like learning geography," thought Alice, as she stood on tiptoe in hopes of being able to see a little further.

For the comparative educator data are at once a blessing and a curse. Without data he runs a constant risk of slipping into metaphysics, where theory can be evaluated only according to the canons of an internal logic. Data provide not merely the original stimulus to the formulation of hypotheses, but they also stand for the real world against which both theory and hypothesis must be tested. But data, like the real world, ramify in infinite complexity. The very quantity of facts available is one of the greatest difficulties of the social sciences in general and of comparative education in particular. Close attention has to be paid to the question of which facts are relevant and meaningful for testing a hypothesis and which are merely distracting.

The distinction was made between facts already collected and those the investigator must collect himself, and at that time the general problems of the former were discussed. If the researcher is forced to collect his own primary data he often still faces similar problems of misrepresentation, unrepresentativeness, incomplete coverage, and so forth. Because collection of one's own material is usually much more expensive than reliance on existing sources, the investigator's options are usually quite limited. Yet collecting one's own data has an obvious advantage: the possibility of establishing the categories most appropriate to the hypotheses to be tested.

Once collected, data must be transformed and adapted to permit comparisons. This requires not only using data to fill out the bare framework of the indicators, but also devising ways to consolidate the data collected, to provide empirical measures of the concepts. Simply adding the measures on each of the indicators may yield a measure of the concept, provided of course that the indicator measures are expressed in the same unit. In this case, each indicator is assumed to have equal importance for quantifying the concept. However, one of the indicators may appear to be more important than another for measuring the concept, perhaps because the data on it are more reliable or because it is supposed to be an outstandingly significant element within the total concept. The problem then arises of choosing weights to attach to the indicators. Sometimes no objective criteria are available to guide weighting, and arbitrary weights are applied on the basis of subjective evaluations. Objective weights are always more desirable, but subjective weights at least make public the nature of the investigator's prejudices.

Model Hypothesis 1

The indicators selected for the first hypothesis are,

EDUCATIONAL-ECONOMIC LEVEL
A. *Educational Level* (C)
    (1) School enrollment ratio for the first and second levels (S)

(2) Public expenditure on education as a percentage of the national income (E)

(3) Percentage of the population aged fifteen years and over that is illiterate (L)

B. *Economic Level*

(4) Per capita gross national product (Y)

All figures for these indicators refer to 1955 or to the nearest year for which data were available.

GROWTH RATE

(5) Average annual growth rate (1957/1958–1964/1965) of per capita output (G)

These indicators call for the use of data readily available from national and international collections.[6] The data on each of these indicators for seventy-one countries are presented in Table 9 (Appendix A).

Table 1 presents the data on each of these indicators for the sixteen high-growth countries selected. Table 2 presents the data for twenty-six low-growth countries. The previous warnings made about limits to the reliability of quantified economic and educational data from governmental and international sources bear repetition. The economic indicators, gross national product per capita, and rates of growth are important statements about the success or failure of a government's economic policy. Consequently, in many countries statistical offices may be encouraged to present them in the most favorable light. In addition, the difficult problem persists of converting figures based on national currencies and the characteristics of national economic systems into internationally comparable statistics. Educational data are also not as straightforward as they may seem at first. Even school enrollment and

[6] For the education indicators, see UNESCO *Statistical Yearbook 1965.* Paris: UNESCO, 1966, pp. 117–137 (enrollment ratios), pp. 342–364 (educational expenditures), pp. 36–46 (illiteracy); for the economic indicators, see Norton Ginsburg, *Atlas of Economic Development.* Chicago: University of Chicago Press, 1957, p. 78, and Agency for International Development, *Gross National Product, Growth Rates, and Trend Data by Region and Country.* Washington, D.C.: Agency for International Development, 1966.

Table 1. Average D-Value of the Group of High-Growth Countries

| | Economic Growth Rate | G.N.P. Per Capita | Educational Indicators | | | | Educational-Economic Profile |
| | | | Enrollment | Expenditure | Illiteracy | Composite Ed. Index | |
	G	Y	S	E	L	C	D
Puerto Rico	12.0	6	2½	1	8	3.8	2.2
Bulgaria	11.4	12	9	10	7	8.7	3.3
Egypt	10.4	16	16	8½	13	12.5	3.5
Rumania	10.3	10	15		5	10.0	0.0
Japan	10.2	13	1	2	2	1.7	11.3
Finland	10.1	2	5	5		5.0	−3.0
Yugoslavia	9.0	11	12	12	10	11.3	−0.3
Israel	7.4	5	4		4	4.0	1.0
Hungary	7.1	8	8	4	3	5.0	3.0
Portugal	6.3	15	14	13	12	13.0	2.0
Greece	6.1	14	10	14	9	11.0	3.0
U. S. S. R.	6.1	4	6	3	1	3.3	0.7
Canada	5.4	1	7	6½		6.8	−5.8
Italy	5.1	7	13	11	6	10.0	−3.0
Denmark	4.8	3	2½	8½		5.5	−2.5
Panama	4.7	9	11	6½	11	9.5	−0.5

(ΣD) Sum of the D's 14.9
(D̄) Average D-Value 0.93

Sources: Data adapted from Norton Ginsburg, *Atlas of Economic Development* (Chicago: University of Chicago Press, 1961), p. 18; UNESCO *Statistical Yearbook 1965* (Paris: UNESCO, 1966), pp. 36–46, 117–137, 342–364.

Table 2. Average D-Value of the Group of Low-Growth Countries

| | Economic Growth Rate | G.N.P. Per Capita | Educational Indicators | | | | Educational-Economic Profile |
| | | | Enrollment | Expenditure | Illiteracy | Composite Ed. Index | |
	G	Y	s	E	L	C	D
Pakistan	2.5	26	22%	18	20	20.2	5.8
El Salvador	2.5	11	14		14	14.0	-3.0
U. S. A.	2.4	1	1	1	1	1.0	0.0
Australia	2.4	2	2	4		3.0	-1.0
Tunisia	2.3	18	19%		21	20.3	-2.3
Guatemala	2.3	15	19½	11	18	16.2	-1.2
Iran	2.1	21½	24		23	23.5	-2.0
Haiti	2.1	23	22%	16%	25	21.3	1.7
Colombia	1.9	6	13	13	10	12.0	-6.0
India	1.8	24	21	8	19	16.0	8.0
Turkey	1.5	8	16	11	16	14.3	-6.3
Ecuador	1.5	12	11½	11	11	11.2	0.8
Venezuela	1.5	3	11½	7	12	10.2	-7.2
Sudan	1.5	21½	26		24	25.0	-3.5
Spain	1.5	10	10	14%	4	9.5	0.5
Bolivia	1.4	25	17		17	17.0	8.0
Brazil	1.3	9	15	6	13	11.3	-2.3
Philippines	1.2	13	5	5	9	6.3	6.7
Chile	1.1	14	7	9	5	7.0	7.0
Honduras	0.9	17	18	16%	15	16.5	0.5
Paraguay	0.8	10	19	14%	7	10.2	9.8
Argentina	0.3	5	3	2	3	2.7	2.3
Costa Rica	0.3	7	5		6	5.5	1.5
Ceylon	0.2	19	5		8	5.3	13.7
Morocco	0.0	16	25	3	22	23.5	-7.5
Uruguay	-1.3	4	8		2	5.0	1.0

Sources: See Table 1.

(ΣD) Sum of the D's 23.0
(D̄) Average D-Value 0.88

literacy figures have their political overtones, and although attendance figures obviously measure different phenomena the definitional gap between the two varies from country to country. Certainly, no matter how honestly or accurately a state may report the number of children enrolled in school, it may be simply impossible to calculate the number of children in the relevant age groups who are not enrolled. The result is that internationally comparable enrollment ratios are extremely elusive.

Yet recognition of the imperfections of data ought not to bring research efforts to a halt. Though far from perfect, the data may offer empirical validation of the concepts under study. Such validation may hardly be necessary for the economic concepts widely used in research, but would be particularly useful to have for the concept of educational level. In each of the selected countries all three indicators are closely interrelated, suggesting the presence of a cluster of educational characteristics for each country, constituting its educational level, and tending to support the belief that the concept is based on more than a merely impressionistic or subjective judgment. The concept appears to have empirical validity. In the preliminary stages of testing a hypothesis, data can be used for no more important purpose than validating the concepts.

When data originally were collected for some other purpose, they may require adaptation before they can be used. Sometimes data are not available for the specific years under consideration. This is especially true of population figures that are, at best, collected at intervals of several years. Because census-taking years and intervals differ from country to country, comparison is often not straightforward. Often the gaps for the period between census-years must be filled in and the commonest way of doing this is to use linear interpolation.[7] Some calculation is also necessary to obtain comparative growth rate figures for a particular period of years

[7] For example, if population figures are given for 1950 and 1960 only, a reasonable estimate of the 1955 population would be the average of the two figures. If population figures are given for 1947 and 1960, however, the simple average of these two will not provide the best estimate for the 1955 population. A better procedure here would be to note that there are thirteen years between 1947 and 1960, and that there are eight years between 1947 and 1955. A good estimate of the 1955 population might then be the 1947 figure plus eight-thirteenths of the increase from 1947 to 1960.

to use in the first model hypothesis. Year-by-year figures of output (gross national product) per capita do exist for the postwar period in many countries, but the investigation requires comparison of average annual rates of economic growth among countries over a specifically defined period. The time period selected was seven years, beginning with 1957/1958 and ending with 1964/1965. The initial figure taken was the average per capita GNP for the two initial years and the final figure was the average for the two end years. Averages for two years were used rather than figures for single years at each end of the period, in order to reduce the error from large year-to-year fluctuations to which growth rates are subject.[8]

The educational indicators used in model hypothesis 1 were also adapted to the purposes of this specific investigation. The three separate indicators of educational level were consolidated to form one composite index (C) for each country (see Tables 1 and 2). Countries were ranked separately on each educational indicator; then, taking each country separately, its rankings on all the indicators were added together. Because data could not be obtained on all three indicators for all countries, the sum of the rankings was divided by the number of indicators on which that country had been ranked. The final figure represents the country's rank on a composite index of educational level. For example, the composite index for a country can be calculated from its separate rankings on indicators S, E, and L. If its ranking on S is 1; on E, 8; and on L, 3—summing these ranks (12) and dividing by 3 gives a composite ranking of educational level equal to 4, an index now comparable with that of other countries.[9]

---

[8] To determine the rate of economic growth, the average per capita GNP for the years 1964/1965 was compared with the average per capita GNP for the years 1957/1958 in constant dollar figures. The rate of growth (r) was calculated using the standard formula:

$$r = 100 \left[\sqrt[n]{\frac{x_n}{x_o}} - 1 \right]$$

where n is the number of time-periods x_o is the value of the GNP per capita at the beginning of the period and x_n the value of the GNP per capita at the end. This is a nonlinear formulation of the average growth rate.

[9] See Appendix A, Table 9, for the basic data on all countries, and Table 10 for the separate and composite rankings of a random sample, based on these data.

A further adjustment demanded by this hypothesis is the construction of an educational-economic profile for each country, that is, a single measure of the relation between its economic and educational levels. Countries can be ranked according to economic level by looking at the figures for annual output of wealth (indicator Y); then this ranking may be compared with the composite ranking of educational level to provide a measure of an individual country's educational-economic profile (D). D is calculated by subtracting the ranking for the educational level from the ranking for the economic level. A country holding, say, fifth rank in economic development and third in educational level achieves a D-value of +2, signifying that its educational ranking is two places higher than its economic ranking. However, a country holding third place in economic development but fifth in education achieves a D-value of −2, signifying that its educational ranking is two places below its economic ranking. This procedure permits the comparison of educational-economic profiles specifically called for by the hypothesis.

Model Hypothesis 2

The data called for by hypothesis 1 were relatively clear, precise, and close to the concepts. Numbers of children enrolled in school or figures of wealth of a nation stand for fairly tangible phenomena, whatever the problems of computation may be. This is not so, however, for the major concepts employed in hypothesis 2, where a very different order of difficulty affects the collection of data. The concepts are far less tangible, they have not been tested by previous research, their validity is still in doubt, and the problem of selecting indicators is formidable. Yet indicators must be chosen to express the concepts of otherworldliness, religiosity, and educational emphasis in quantitative terms if they are to be handled in empirical investigation.

The indicators selected for the second hypothesis are,

IDEOLOGY
  A. *Otherworldliness* (O)
      (1) Importance of belief in the hereafter (H)
      (2) Importance of a priesthood and the extent to which it is differentiated from the lay population (P)
      (3) Extent of ritualistic content (X)
      (4) Degree of emphasis on monasticism (M)
      (5) Attention given to the problems of this world (W)
  B. *Religiosity* (R)
      (6) Constitutional relation of the religion to the state (C)
      (7) Status of religious instruction in the public school system (I)
      (8) Proportion of the population affiliated to the dominant religion (A)
EDUCATION
  C. *Theoretical vs. Practical Emphasis* (T/P)
      (9) Ratio of enrollments in the natural sciences to enrollments in engineering at the third level (S/E)
      (10) Ratio of enrollments in general education to enrollments in vocational education at the second level (G/V)

As regards enrollments in the natural sciences and engineering (S and E), figures for a two-year period were taken (1960/1961 and 1961/1962 or the nearest years for which data were available). Two-year figures were preferred over figures for a single year to dampen the effect of large year-to-year fluctuations in enrollments. As regards enrollments in general secondary and vocational secondary education, figures for single years (1960/1961 or the nearest year for which data were available) were employed.

To collect data on the otherworldliness characteristics of a religious ideology, the investigator must consult primary and secondary literature in each religion. For example, the sacred books of the religion will be a primary source for determining the emphasis on belief in the hereafter. Here, the technique of content-analysis may be profitably employed.[10] Secondary, nonsacred material may

[10] Techniques of content-analysis have been much developed in recent years. See McClelland, *The Achieving Society,* chap. III, for one example; also Merritt and Rokkan (eds.), *op. cit.,* pp. 565–566, provides a bibliography of content-analyses in various fields.

be consulted to assess the importance of the priesthood, ritual, and monasticism in the religion. In similar fashion, description and analyses of the role of religion in national life will furnish the data for indicators of religiosity. Some of this material is already cast in comparative form, but the bulk of it is not. Certainly there is everything to be gained from consulting the authorities that already exist, because they provide invaluable interpretations of the primary, sacred texts, and because of the saving of time and effort. For the educational indicators, data on enrollment ratios are generally available in standard form on national bases.[11]

Before converting the data into quantified and comparable terms, some of the important reservations and qualifications already made must be applied to the collection and adaptation of data for this particular investigation.

Since more than one type of Islamic, Buddhist, or Christian ideology may be found among the nations of the world, a major problem is raised when the otherworldliness of a given religious ideology is equated with the world-outlook of a specific nation. This procedure ignores the variations of a religious ideology, both within and among regions. The difficulty is partly met in two ways. First, the religiosity factor of a nation is used to weight the otherworldliness factor of the dominant religion. By taking into account

[11] For the education indicators, see UNESCO *Statistical Yearbook, 1965*. Paris: UNESCO, 1966, UNESCO, *World Survey of Education*, vol. IV. New York: UNESCO, 1966; *The World of Learning 1966–67*. London: Europa Publications, 1967; and the *Europa Yearbook 1967: A World Survey and Directory of Countries and International Organizations*, 2 vols. London: Europa Publications, 1967. See also the report of the Committee on Higher Education, *Higher Education*. London: H.M.S.O., 1964 (the Robbins Report), Appendix Five of which is entitled "Higher Education in Other Countries." This volume not only provides some enrollment figures by subject for selected countries, but also refers to additional sources. Other sources of enrollment figures by subject studied usually may be found in the statistical publications of each national ministry of education. For secondary sources on religion, church and state, see: A. C. Bouquet, *Comparative Religion*. Baltimore, Md.: Penguin Books, 1962; J. Lloyd Mecham, *Church and State in Latin America*, Revised edition. Chapel Hill, N.C.: University of North Carolina Press, 1966; Fred R. Von Der Mehden, *Religion and Nationalism in Southeast Asia*. Madison, Wis.: The University of Wisconsin Press, 1963; Joachim Wach, *Sociology of Religion*. Chicago: The University of Chicago Press, 1944; and George Z. F. Bereday and Joseph A. Lauwerys (eds.), *The World Yearbook of Education, 1966*. New York: Harcourt, Brace and World, 1966.

the constitutional status of the major religion, its place in public school education and the proportion of the population affiliated formally to the religion, a measure may be devised (albeit a rough one) of the power and pervasiveness of the religious ideology in the nation. The second device, attempted in the case of the wealthier countries in this investigation, is to use denominations of Protestantism as the basis for sampling countries, rather than the undifferentiated category of Protestantism.

All the difficulties usually associated with collecting and interpreting data are compounded in this investigation. Comparable data for all the indicators and for all the religions included are difficult to collect and special problems of interpretation are raised. For example, it was intended to include some rating of the tolerance accorded to minority religions within individual countries as an indicator of religiosity, but this proved to be extremely difficult to assess, and the indicator was abandoned. Moreover, even when data were available for several indicators, problems of interpretation arose. Rating a religion on the dimension of, say, ritual is not easy (is the Catholic religion more ritualistic than the Jewish?). Though not altogether satisfactory, one device to meet this problem is to rate on the basis of the judgment of, say, three evaluators rather than one, in an attempt to reduce arbitrariness.

Some adaptation of the raw data is necessary to translate a mass of impressionistic and heterogenous data about the otherworldliness content of various religious ideologies into a standardized form permitting comparison between religions. For each indicator of otherworldliness (H, P, X, M, and W), each religion is ranked within its group. Higher numbers signify greater degrees of otherworldliness. An otherworldliness score (O) can then be obtained for each religion by summing the numerical values of the separate indicators. Table 3 gives the numerical values assigned to the several indicators for each religion and the final otherworldliness index.[12]

This simple method of quantifying the data results in a total otherworldliness score for each country. These aggregates are not

---

[12] See Appendix B for examples of the rationale for assigning numbers to each religion.

Table 3. **Rankings on Indicators of Otherworldliness**

	Hereafter	Priesthood	Ritual	Monasticism	This World	Otherworldliness
	H	P	X	M	W	O
Poor countries						
Catholic (Bolivia, Peru)	3	3	3	2	1	12
Hindu (India)	4	4	3	4	4	19
Islamic (Pakistan, Egypt)	2	1	3	1	2	9
Buddhist (Thailand, Burma)	1	2	1	3	3	10
Rich countries						
Catholic (France, Ireland, Italy)	5	5	4.5	5	5	24.5
Anglican (England)	2	4	3	4	3	16
Lutheran (Sweden)	4	3	2	2.5	4	15.5
Presbyterian (Scotland)	3	2	1	2.5	2	10.5
Jewish (Israel)	1	1	4.5	1	1	8.5

measured quantities; that is, a score of 12 does not indicate twice as much otherworldliness as a score of 6. The numerical size of intervals between scores has no significance in absolute terms, but only relative significance. This mode of adapting the data merely permits religious ideologies to be ranked on a scale of otherworldliness.

In Table 4 the data on religiosity are presented in quantified form. However, whereas the measures on the indicators of otherworldliness were rankings, the measures here are not. Only two values are used for each indicator. For C, if the country has an established church, a value of 1 is assigned; and, if not, 0. For I, if religious instruction is given in the public schools, a value of 1 is assigned; if not, 0. But for the third indicator, percentage of the population affiliated to the dominant church (A), a value of 2 is assigned for a percentage over 90, and a value of 1 for a percentage under 90. The rationale for this different procedure, which implicitly weights indicator A more heavily than either C or I, is to take cognizance of the fact that, in all the countries selected, over 80 per cent of the population adheres to the dominant faith. Therefore for all these countries the minimum religiosity score appropriate is 1, rather than 0. The final religiosity score of each country is used to weight the otherworldliness score of its dominant religion. This results in an adjusted (weighted) index of otherworldliness ($R \times O$).

The remaining data on the two education indicators are presented in Table 5. The two sets of enrollment figures are converted into two ratios (S/E and G/V), which are then multiplied to achieve a single index of the theoretical versus practical emphasis in education for each country (T/P).

The lack of data for Scotland provides an example of a difficult and quite common problem in empirical work. One of the ratios, G/V, required to calculate T/P is missing for Scotland. The country has no vocational secondary schools, and the table indicates that the ratio G/V is not applicable, for the excellent mathematical reason that

$$\frac{\text{enrollment in general secondary education}}{\text{zero}}$$

Table 4. Religiosity and Adjusted Index of Otherworldliness

	Church State Relation	Religious Instruction in Schools	Church Affiliation	Religiosity	Other-worldliness	Adjusted Index of Otherworldliness
	C	I	A	R	O	RxO
Poor countries						
CATHOLIC						
Bolivia	1	0	2	3	12	36
Peru	1	1	2	4	12	48
HINDU						
India	0	0	1	1	19	19
ISLAMIC						
Pakistan	1	1	1	3	9	27
Egypt	1	1	2	4	9	36
BUDDHIST						
Thailand	1	1	2	4	10	40
Burma	1	1	1	3	10	30
Rich countries						
CATHOLIC						
France	0	0	1	1	24.5	24.5
Ireland	0	1	2	3	24.5	73.5
Italy	1	1	2	4	24.5	98
ANGLICAN (England)	1	1	1	3	16	48
LUTHERAN (Sweden)	1	1	2	4	15.5	62
PRESBYTERIAN (Scotland)	1	1	1	3	10.5	31.5
JEWISH (Israel)	1	1	1	3	8.5	25.5

Table 5. Educational Emphasis: Theoretical vs. Practical

	Enrollments*		Ratio	Enrollments†		Ratio	Educational Emphasis S/E x G/V
	Natural Science	Engineering		General Secondary	Vocational Secondary		
	s	E	S/E	G	v	G/V	T/P
Poor countries							
CATHOLIC							
Bolivia	.57	1.5	.37	50.6	8.9	5.64	2.09
Peru	7.53	7.9	.96	158.9	39.4	4.04	3.88
HINDU							
India	632.9	94.7	6.68	8,989.3	282.7	31.80	212.0
ISLAMIC							
Pakistan	43.4	6.7	6.44	1,493.5	12.3	121.9	784.6
Egypt	13.3	34.7	.38	448.4	126.4	3.55	1.35
BUDDHIST							
Thailand	3.5	3.2	1.11	270.8	76.1	3.55	3.92
Burma	10.3	1.6	6.30	307.0	2.9	104.6	658.9
Rich countries							
CATHOLIC							
France	217.1	50.6	4.19	1,880.7	443.0	4.25	17.8
Ireland	3.1	1.5	2.15	87.0	31.4	2.77	5.95
Italy	50.7	42.0	1.21	1,767.2	503.7	3.52	4.26
ANGLICAN (England)	54.1	58.0	.93	3,247.2	1,452.5	2.24	2.08
LUTHERAN (Sweden)	13.2	11.7	1.12	219.6	184.7	1.18	1.32
PRESBYTERIAN (Scotland)	8.2	9.4	.87	295.8	0	n.a.	.76
JEWISH (Israel)	4.3	5.0	.86	52.7	23.7	2.23	1.94

* In thousands. Sum of two years, 1960/1961 and 1961/1962, or the nearest for which data are available.
† In thousands, 1960/1961.
n.a. = not applicable.
Source: Data from *UNESCO Statistical Yearbook 1965* (Paris: UNESCO, 1966).

is a meaningless expression. Hence, the method used to calculate T/P for the other countries cannot be employed here. There are a number of alternatives. The first is to look more closely at the Scottish system of secondary education and compute what fraction of secondary school students were enrolled in vocational education *courses* in the general secondary schools, and use this ratio in place of one based on enrollment in *institutions*. This would certainly be worth doing if the results of the investigation show that country as an obvious exception to otherwise clean and decisive findings. A second possibility, when there are anomalous cases, is to omit the offending country, but this may invite the challenge that the cases have been handpicked to produce a desired result. The third possibility is simply to assume that Scotland's S/E ratio (.87) can be used to represent her G/V ratio as well. This is, in fact, the approach used in Table 5. It is open to many objections (it almost certainly underestimates the actual theoretical emphasis in Scottish education), but it has the merit of simplicity.

Manipulating the Data

> *"Consider your verdict," the King said to the jury.*
> *"Not yet, not yet!" the Rabbit hastily interrupted.*
> *"There's a great deal to come before that!"*

Manipulation of the data is the attempt to clarify the relationships among them. They are organized and presented so that statements are possible about the validity of the hypothesis. The options for manipulating and presenting the data are usually numerous, ranging from simple correlations to their use in testing complex models expressed in mathematical terms. Nevertheless, it is not so much the sophistication of the techniques employed to analyze and present the data, as the basic validity and reliability of the data themselves and the investigator's wisdom and common sense in using them that determines the value of the results.[1] Moreover, some data

---

[1] The investigator's wisdom and judgment in handling the data are in some circles colloquially known as the ש-factor, or שכל-factor. The authors are indebted to their colleague, Seymour Warkov, for drawing this handy term to their attention.

lend themselves to elaborate manipulation, while others have already been so transformed from the original "facts" that it would be better not to subject them to further complicated handling.[2]

Model Hypothesis 1

Some of the simpler techniques of manipulating data are illustrated in the following discussion of each of the two model hypotheses. In the treatment of hypothesis 1, averages of D-values and growth rates for groups of countries are compared. Tables 1 and 2 brought together the data, adjusted and adapted to the special purposes of this investigation. They are now used to make possible some statements about the validity of the hypothesis. Table 1 presented some simple manipulations for a group of high growth countries, and Table 2 dealt with low growth countries. If the hypothesis is to be confirmed, one would expect to find a higher proportion of countries with a positive D-value (more favorable educational-economic profile) among the high-growth countries than among the low-growth countries. This is indeed the case, but the difference is far from impressive. Of the sixteen high-growth countries, ten have positive D-values (62 per cent); of the twenty six low-growth countries, fourteen have positive D-values (54 per cent).

A more precise test of the hypothesis is to calculate the average D-values of the two groups of countries and compare them. If the hypothesis is to be confirmed, countries exhibiting high levels of economic growth should have, on average, higher D-values than countries exhibiting low levels of growth. At the foot of the last columns of Tables 1 and 2 the D-values of the high- and low-growth countries are summed separately, and averaged. Although

[2] There are many textbooks dealing with the problems involved in the statistical manipulation of data. Since detailed discussion of these techniques is not called for in the present volume, the reader is referred to Kerlinger, *Foundations of Behavioral Research* and Moroney, *Facts from Figures, inter alia.*

the high-growth figure is greater, again the difference is small (about 6 per cent) and certainly not sufficient to confirm the hypothesis.

But if no significant difference of average D-value can be found between the two groups, it is conceivable that differences may emerge *within* each of the two groups considered separately. Tables 6 and 7 relate respectively to the high- and low-growth groups, and compare, separately within each sample, educational-economic profiles and subsequent rates of economic growth. The first column of figures reproduces the D-values given in Tables 1 and 2. Then there follow two columns in which the growth rates are entered (unweighted). The first lists the growth rates for those countries with a positive educational-economic profile (D is greater than 0),

Table 6. **High-Growth Countries. A Comparison of Educational-Economic Profiles and Subsequent Economic Growth**

	Educational-Economic Profile	Growth Rates by Groups			
		Unweighted		Weighted	
	D	D > 0	D < 0	D > 0	D < 0
Puerto Rico	2.2	12.0		26.0	
Bulgaria	3.3	11.4		38.0	
Egypt	3.5	10.4		36.4	
Rumania	0.0				
Japan	11.3	10.2		115.6	
Finland	−3.0		10.1		30.5
Yugoslavia	−0.3		9.0		3.0
Israel	1.0	7.4		7.4	
Hungary	3.0	7.1		21.3	
Portugal	2.0	6.3		12.6	
Greece	3.0	6.1		18.3	
U.S.S.R.	0.7	6.1		4.3	
Canada	−5.8		5.4		31.1
Italy	−3.0		5.1		15.3
Denmark	−2.5		4.8		12.0
Panama	−0.5		4.7		2.4
	ΣG = 77.0	39.1	279.9	94.1	
	$\overline{\text{G}}$ = 8.6	6.5	9.3	6.3	
	(Sum of the weights)		(30.0)	(15.1)	

Table 7. **Low-Growth Countries. A Comparison of Educational-Economic Profiles and Subsequent Economic Growth**

	Educational-Economic Profile	Growth Rates by Groups			
		Unweighted		Weighted	
	D	D $>$ 0	D $<$ 0	D $>$ 0	D $<$ 0
Pakistan	5.8	2.5		14.6	
El Salvador	−3.0		2.5		7.5
U. S. A.	0.0				
Australia	−1.0		2.4		2.4
Tunisia	−2.3		2.3		5.2
Guatemala	−1.2		2.3		2.7
Iran	−2.0		2.1		4.3
Haiti	1.7	2.1		3.5	
Colombia	−6.0		1.9		11.4
India	8.0	1.8		14.4	
Turkey	−6.3		1.5		9.5
Ecuador	0.8	1.5		1.3	
Venezuela	−7.2		1.5		10.8
Sudan	−3.5		1.5		5.3
Spain	0.5	1.5		0.8	
Bolivia	8.0	1.4		11.2	
Brazil	−2.3		1.3		3.0
Philippines	6.7	1.2		8.0	
Chile	7.0	1.1		7.7	
Honduras	0.5	0.9		0.5	
Paraguay	9.8	0.8		7.9	
Argentina	2.3	0.3		0.7	
Costa Rica	1.5	0.3		0.5	
Ceylon	13.7	0.2		2.7	
Morocco	−7.5		0.0		0.0
Uruguay	−1.0		−1.3		−1.3
		18.0	73.8	60.8	
		1.5	1.1	1.4	
	(Sum of the weights)			(66.3)	(43.8)

$$\Sigma G = 15.2$$
$$\overline{G} = 1.2$$

Sources: Data adapted from Norton Ginsburg, *Atlas of Economic Development* (Chicago: University of Chicago Press, 1961), p. 18; UNESCO *Statistical Yearbook 1965* (Paris: UNESCO, 1966), pp. 36–46, 117–137, 342–364.

and the second column lists the growth rates for those countries with a negative profile (D is less than 0). Each column is summed separately, and the totals divided by the number of countries summed. Thus, the figure 8.6 represents the average growth rate of countries with a positive educational-economic profile, and the figure 6.5 the average growth rate of countries with a negative profile (for the sample of high-growth countries only). In Table 7 similar manipulation for the countries in the low-growth category yields an average growth rate of 1.2 for the countries with a positive D, and 1.5 for countries with a negative D. These results make it possible to make some statements about the validity of the hypothesis.

What do the results mean? In the high-growth countries there is a considerable difference between the average growth experience of the positive D and the negative D countries. The group that had a favorable educational-economic profile exhibited subsequent growth rates almost one-third higher than countries with unfavorable profiles. As for the low-growth countries, it is apparent that the relationship asserted in the hypothesis is not merely not confirmed, but is actually disconfirmed: the average growth rate for the countries where the educational level is in advance of the economic level is one-fifth *lower* than the average growth rate of the countries with a negative educational-economic profile.

Further manipulation may help to draw additional meaning from the data. Obviously, it is not entirely satisfactory to ignore the fact that the measures of the profiles (the D-values) differ considerably. Taking just two categories, positive D and negative D, fails to take into account the full range of differences within each category. For example, among the high-growth countries with positive D, the range stretches from Japan with D = 11.3 to the U. S. S. R. with D = 0.7; and among the countries with negative D, the range is from Yugoslavia with D = −0.3, to Canada with D = −5.8. But it may be reasonably assumed, following the implications of the hypothesis, that rates of subsequent economic growth will be affected not only by the presence or absence of a favorable educational-economic profile, but by its magnitude. This consideration may be taken into account by a simple weighting procedure, which appears in the two final columns of each table. Countries with positive and negative D are again handled separately, but now each country's growth rate is multiplied by its respective D-value. Thus, among the high growth countries, Japan's growth rate of 10.2 is multiplied by its D-value of 11.3, resulting in a weighted growth rate of 115.6; while the U. S. S. R.'s growth rate of 6.1 is multiplied by its D-value of 0.7, to produce a weighted growth rate of 4.3. This manipulation is designed to recognize the different relations of low D-values and high D-values to subsequent growth rates. After weighting the growth rates for each country in this manner, the columns are again summed separately, and average growth rates computed by dividing each total by the total of the weights for that category of countries. The same weighting, summing, and averaging procedures were applied to the figures for the low-growth countries.

Again, what do the results mean? In the case of the high-growth countries, the difference in the average growth rates is now even more pronounced than with unweighted measures: countries with positive D-values achieved an average rate of subsequent growth equal to 9.3 per cent per annum; whereas countries with negative D-values had an average rate of growth equal to 6.3. For the high-growth countries in this period, the hypothesis is again confirmed, and now considerably more definitely.

As for the low-growth countries, the results after weighting give an average subsequent growth rate of 1.1 per cent per annum for countries with a favorable educational-economic profile, and a growth rate of 1.4 for the countries with an unfavorable profile. Notice that the weighted result moderately sharpens the distinctions. The hypothesis is just a little more strongly disconfirmed than before: countries where educational level is high relative to economic level achieve a subsequent average growth rate that is one fifth to one quarter lower than countries with a negative educational-economic profile.

Model Hypothesis 2

Table 8 juxtaposes the indexes of T/P and R × O so that the rankings on each of these measures may be compared, country by

Table 8. Rankings on Educational Emphasis and Otherworldliness (Adjusted) Compared

			Rankings	
	Educational Emphasis	Adjusted Other-worldliness	Educational Emphasis	Adjusted Other-worldliness
	T/P	RₓO	T/P	RₓO
Poor countries				
CATHOLIC				
Bolivia	2.09	36	6	3.5
Peru	3.88	48	5	1
HINDU				
India	212.	19	3	7
ISLAMIC				
Pakistan	784.6	27	1	6
Egypt	1.35	36	7	3.5
BUDDHIST				
Thailand	3.92	40	4	2
Burma	658.9	30	2	5
Rich countries				
CATHOLIC				
France	17.8	24.5	1	7
Ireland	5.95	73.5	2	2
Italy	4.26	98	3	1
ANGLICAN (England)	2.08	48	4	4
LUTHERAN (Sweden)	1.32	62	6	3
PRESBYTERIAN (Scotland)	0.76	31.5	7	5
JEWISH (Israel)	1.94	25.5	5	6

Source: Based on Tables 4 and 5.

country. For the hypothesis to be confirmed totally and without exception, the rank orders for the two variables would have to be identical for each country. However, it is immediately apparent from Table 8 that this result has not been achieved, and that the hypothesis is unsupported for both groups of countries. The rankings suggest that there is, at most, a bare suspicion of an inverse relation between otherworldliness and theoretical emphasis in education among the group of poor countries and no discernible relation at all between these two variables among the richer countries. Thus,

POOR COUNTRIES		RICH COUNTRIES	
Otherworldliness (O)	*Theoretical Emphasis* (T/P)	*Otherworldliness* (O)	*Theoretical Emphasis* (T/P)
Peru	Pakistan	Italy	France
Thailand	Burma	Ireland	Ireland
Bolivia	India	Sweden	Italy
Egypt	Thailand	England	England
Burma	Peru	Scotland	Israel
Pakistan	Bolivia	Israel	Sweden
India	Egypt	France	Scotland

More ↓ *Less*

By computing correlation coefficients for the ranks it is possible to express all this information compactly. For the poor countries r (the rank correlation coefficient) equals $-.58$; for the rich countries r equals $+.018$.

17

Implications of the Results

"Tut, tut, child!" said the Duchess. "Everything's got a moral, if only you can find it."

In science as much importance is attached to process as to results. Whereas specific conclusions are, of course, always valuable, often the methods of achieving the results and their implications for further inquiry are of greater interest. An investigation by no means says the final word on a problem when particular results have been obtained, for they report the consequences of specific ways of manipulating the data, and immediately raise the questions, are there alternative manipulations possible that might achieve a more rigorous test of the hypothesis and, can the test of the hypothesis be improved by employing further data or a different sample of cases?

Moreover, given certain results, the investigator must try to relate them to findings of other relevant studies. Whether his findings tend to confirm or contradict those made by others, this procedure is valuable. Confirmation strengthens the confidence one may have in the findings, both old and new; conflicting results immediately raise problems calling for further investigation. The results must also be related back to the theory from which the hypothesis sprang. One of the most important implications of a particular set of results is that theory is either strengthened or weakened, extended in its explanatory power, or limited. Just as well-mounted investigation will help identify gaps, obscurities, and ambiguities in the data, well-founded conclusions will help identify gaps, obscurities, and ambiguities in the theory relevant to the hypothesis.

The heuristic value of an investigation also resides in the implications of results, pointing toward fuller and more general explanations. Very often a given problem is first investigated extremely simplistically: a limited number of variables is included, and a very simple relationship between them is hypothesized. The results from these first attempts may point the way to studies that take into account a larger number of variables and more complex relationships. What began as an elementary study of covariance between a pair of phenomena may end in probings into the complex processes at work in an entire sector of education and society.

The results of an investigation may suggest yet another set of implications: those associated with policy. Conclusions about a particular problem in education may suggest action to improve the situation. In the final accounting, the policy-making implications are often considered to be the most important of all. But extreme caution is mandatory. It is not uncommon in education (as in the social sciences) to propose a course of action based on the results of research that may be exceptionally well founded in itself and may have satisfactorily established the existence of a particular relationship. But in the absence of a sufficiently well-developed theory into which the particular results can be fitted, action based on them may be doomed to failure. Unfortunately, in the social sciences powerful and reliable theory is exceptionally difficult to achieve and action undertaken on the basis of imperfectly developed theory is not only premature, but dangerous. The mark of a powerful theory is that it enables us to make "if-then" statements with confidence. Yet theory must reach a rather advanced level of sophistication and explanatory power before it can provide a basis for policy actions, the outcomes of which can be predicted with a reasonable degree of confidence. If theory is imperfectly developed, the specific conditions under which an "if-then" statement will have validity are not known: the full array of important factors that will influence outcomes is not yet identified and the complex processes of their interaction not yet understood. Policies based on imperfect theory are apt to produce highly unexpected results, and when reliable theory is lacking intuitively based action may well prove more useful in achieving the ends desired.

Model Hypothesis 1

In view of the results obtained, implications immediately arise for alternative ways of testing hypothesis 1. Because it has been shown that the relationship posited in the hypothesis has been affirmed by the sample of high-growth countries and rejected and even contradicted in the case of the low-growth countries, obviously it is necessary to investigate countries in the middle range of economic growth. Another way of testing the hypothesis is to group countries on some basis other than their growth rates. Economic level is clearly a crucial factor, so it might be advisable to rerun the inquiry, grouping countries according to their economic levels (for example, gross national product per capita, degree of industrialization, degree of urbanization, and so on). In Appendix A there are examples of two different ways of selecting cases and of manipulating data for further testing the hypothesis.

Better data, too, often can improve a study. In general there are two ways data can be improved: more accurate versions of figures already incorporated into the investigation, or more refined measures of the relevant variables. For example, educational level (C) has been largely measured by indexes of input (enrollment ratios and expenditure on education). Only one output measure (literacy) was used, and a rather crude one at that. Further investigation based on improved measures of educational level and focusing as much on the quality of educational output as on its quantity might generate more authoritative results.

The results obtained from the actual investigation of hypothesis 1 appear to demonstrate a relationship between educational-economic profile and subsequent economic growth that varies according to the economic levels of the countries. The results are not inconsistent with the findings of others who have asserted that the relationship between education and economic growth differs under different economic conditions. Thus, Anderson and Bowman found that increases in literacy accompanied increases in income per head both in the poorer and in the richer countries, but that there was a large intermediate range of countries in which increases in literacy and increases in wealth seemed to exhibit no systematic relationship.[1] Nor are the results inconsistent with other findings indicating that in general the poor countries are poor because they have not yet learned how to make the best use of their physical resources. The findings for hypothesis 1 extend the reach of such a dictum to include some indication that poor countries also use investment in education inefficiently. Certainly the results obtained raise questions about any simplistic explanations of the relationship between a country's investment effort (whether in the formation of physical or educational capital) and its future chances of economic growth. It is obvious that much remains to be learned about the role of education in the economic development of very poor countries.

The exact process by which educational investment does or does not stimulate subsequent economic growth remains unclear. The pattern and timing of educational expansion along with cultural factors (such as attitudes towards modernization) may be important and require further investigation. Not until these and other influential factors have been explored and their relationships clarified can it be claimed that there exists any theory with substantial explanatory power in this area. Until such a time, the policy implications of the particular findings of hypothesis 1 are meager. He would be an ill-advised planner who took the particular results ob-

[1] See Chap. 6.

tained as any indication that poor countries should curtail their educational efforts, or rich countries seek to expand them. Nor do the results provide any guide at all to profitable specific ways of curtailing or expanding educational provision in any country. Their greatest value, it would seem, lies in pointing toward needed areas of research by suggesting a host of further hypotheses for subsequent investigation.

Model Hypothesis 2

Even more than in the case of hypothesis 1, the results obtained here must be handled with extreme caution. But notwithstanding all the reservations already made about the concepts and the data, the results achieved presumably have some meaning, however elusive. Consequently it is worth searching for their implications. Obviously, much remains to be done to improve the conceptualization of the problem stated in the hypothesis, and the data used to test it stand in great need of refinement.

Because the original hypothesis was neither confirmed nor disconfirmed, the investigator might be encouraged to turn the hypothesis around and try to test the relationship between, say, secularism in national life and educational emphasis, using indicators other than those already employed for otherworldliness to measure the new variable. Secularism may be a more easily operationalized concept than otherworldliness and may yield more definite results.

There are many ways to improve the data. Instead of relying on secondary sources and interpretations of sacred documents, original primary data might be gathered. Questionnaires might be administered to the faithful, and trained observers might record the behavior of the laity and the clergy. Personal observation may provide relevant data on the priesthood and its training. All this information would provide better data needed for more precise quantification of the otherworldliness of a religion. As regards the measurement of the educational emphasis, it would be highly desirable to have data not merely on enrollments in types of courses or schools, but on the theoretical versus practical content of curricula in primary and secondary schools. One way to achieve this would be to look at the allocation of school time among the different subjects. A further refinement, and one much more difficult to accomplish, would be to determine whether the approach in the teaching of representative subjects aims at theoretical understanding or practical application, and to quantify this dimension.

Because the results of this particular study were so indeterminate, bases for sampling other than the ones used ought to be considered for a more rigorous test of the hypothesis. One basis mentioned in Chapter 14 appears to have potential: to compare single educational institutions or school systems associated with different religious ideologies located within one country. This procedure might make available much sharper data and possibly hold constant important national variables. This would, of course, imply abandoning the cross-national aspect of the study but its comparative nature nevertheless would be retained.

Another set of implications has to do with the relationship between the results and the very general and vague theory that helped generate the hypothesis. It was recognized early in the investigation that there was a relationship between a country's level of wealth and the dominant religion. For example, Islamic, Buddhist, and Hindu countries are poor and most of the Christian countries are rich. Because of this, countries were deliberately parcelled into two groups, the rich and the poor, and analyzed separately. Inspection of the T/P indexes listed in Table 8 reveals that all countries except Scotland are recorded as emphasizing theoretical over practical studies, but that some do this much more than others. It might be worthwhile trying to hold level of wealth constant within a large group of rich countries and within a large group of poor countries in order to isolate the specific effect of otherworldliness, uncontaminated by the possible effects of level of wealth. One simple way is to pair countries at roughly the same level of wealth, discriminating between them as to otherworldliness, and examining the educational emphasis. This would then be repeated for as many pairs as possible, and the results tabulated, in order to see whether the more otherworldly country in each pair generally had a greater or lesser theoretical emphasis.

Given that the results obtained have some validity, they offer no confirmation for the hypothesis; nor do they succeed in disconfirming it. The question raised by the hypothesis remains open. A proposition that appeared eminently reasonable is not supported by empirical test. It may be that a hidden factor is operating, one which has not been recognized and incorporated explicitly into the analysis; alternatively it may be that the original theoretical framework was inadequate and a new one will have to be constructed to make sense of the results. Such heuristic implications are undoubtedly the most important fruits of the scientific approach to comparative study.

Part Four

CONCLUSION

"No wise fish would go anywhere without a porpoise."

18

Toward a Science
of Comparative Education

> *"Cheshire-Puss,"* [*Alice*] *began . . . "Would you tell me, please, which way I ought to go from here?"*
>
> *"That depends a good deal on where you want to get to," said the Cat.*

When Alice went on to explain that she did not much care where she went, the Cheshire Cat interrupted her sharply to say that, in that case, it did not really matter which path she took. But then Alice continued, ". . . so long as I get *somewhere*." The Cheshire Cat pointed out that this was no serious problem. If only she walked long enough, she was bound to get somewhere.

Unfortunately, the Cat's logic is only apparent. Alice, like any traveler, conceivably might end up nowhere rather than somewhere. She might cover the countryside only to arrive back at her point of departure, or she might stumble upon new places without ever realizing she had done so. However, most damaging is the probability that, after having been somewhere, Alice would be quite unable to state where it was, how she got there, whether she had taken the best route, or what conceivable use the whole journey had been to her or anyone else. The analogy to research in cross-national data is obvious.

The exotic lure of foreign places, manners, and customs is overwhelming. The simple acts of going and seeing for oneself and the unpredictable joys of serendipity become their own rewards; and surely if we visit abroad enough, read diligently, and cooperate with others of like interest, comparative study must get somewhere. Yet the painful truth is that it may not get anywhere at all. It may simply go around in a circle, repeating over and over again the same stale "facts," refurbished from time to time. Or comparative study may stumble over important findings, but have no notion how they fit in to the surrounding territory, how exactly they were arrived at, or how to make the best use of them now that they have been discovered. It has been the single argument of this book that, armed with the question, "Where do I wish to go?" and intent on using and improving a map to reach his destination, the wandering scholar in cross-national data greatly betters his chances of undertaking a journey that will be valuable both to himself and to his colleagues in the field.

At some stage of development, most disciplines have had to give thought to several related questions. What material and which problems lie squarely within the purview of the discipline, and which lie outside? What, if any, are the characteristic methods of the field? And what are the criteria for determining whether a piece of work in the field is good, bad, or indifferent? Comparative education today is forced hard against these question, and twist and turn as they may, comparative educators have to try to provide answers that are satisfactory to themselves, to their colleagues in adjacent areas of education studies, and to colleagues working in the social sciences.

Much of this book has been devoted to an attempt to give some answer to the first two questions. The territory of comparative education has been defined as the intersection of the social sciences, education studies, and the cross-national dimension, so that the hallmark of work properly claiming to be comparative education is that it lies neatly within that intersection. In addition, it has been argued, the characteristic methods of the field presently can be specified no more rigorously than that they are (or should be) derived from the social sciences. But the third question, which demands the establishment of criteria for the evaluation of work in comparative education, has remained largely unanswered, both in the larger world of work in comparative education and so far in this volume.

Such criteria are most urgently needed everywhere in the field: by those who do research and write in comparative education, by journal editors who must judge whether or not to publish work submitted, by those who teach the subject and by students seeking to learn, and not least by planners wishing to base decisions for the reform and development of educational systems at least partly on the findings of comparative education. Yet it is no secret that the minimum criteria simply do not exist. Writing in the field tends to be largely descriptive, anecdotal, or hortatory. Publishing is indiscriminate, and though every genre of work is represented the factual and narrative items vastly outnumber the carefully explanatory. Courses in comparative education are characteristically haphazard and eclectic; beginning courses in comparative education offered in colleges and universities provide students with widely dissimilar treatments of the field, in both subject matter and method of approach—a phenomenon not to be found in, say, American History I, or Chemistry I. And woe to the planner, either national or international, who relies on the findings of comparative education to sustain his search for some guiding principles of educational development, for he will come away from a survey of the literature with very little of value.

This absence of generally accepted criteria against which to evaluate work in comparative education can best be explained by reference to the antecedents of the field. Until quite recently it has been dominated by simple curiosity about foreign lands and customs, or by a desire to borrow foreign practices, or by the hope of promoting international brotherhood and cooperation. These motives, while highly laudable, are inadequate bases to sustain a field of study. Only since the beginning of the century has the task of explanation moved to the center of the stage, and historical and philosophical methods been used to interpret educational and social phenomena with great perceptivity, scholarliness, and intuitive insight. But even here a consistent and defensible methodology has been largely lacking. Comparative education for the most part has not had as its goal the provision of validated explanations, nor have its results been assessed, as a matter of routine, for their predictive value. In short, the real potential of comparative study has gone largely unexploited. Instead of using cross-national data to test the validity of statements about relationships between education and society, comparative education has for too long remained simply a pleasantly exotic field in which those who happened to have some experience of foreign education can busy themselves.

The development of the social sciences along empirical lines has, however, opened up a new arena for comparative work. Many propositions already validated in individual (case-study) situations are prime candidates for cross-national testing of their wider applicability, while many other propositions simply cannot be tested at all without recourse to comparative models and data. Most important of all, perhaps, the method of work enjoined by an empirical social science approach provides the criteria needed for evaluating work in comparative education. Systematic, controlled, empirical, and (wherever possible) quantitative investigation of explicitly stated hypotheses is the hallmark of the contemporary social sciences; it needs to become a modus operandi of those who would call themselves comparative educators, too.

To the extent that the investigator in cross-national research is crystal-clear in his own mind and makes quite clear to his readers, precisely which hypothetical proposition he is testing, he furnishes himself with a focus for research and his readers with a clear guide to understanding the implications of the results achieved. However, to the extent that work using cross-national educational data is unsystematic, lacks explicit controls, appeals for proof to authority or intuition rather than to the facts, and ignore possibilities of quantification of variables it is poor social science and therefore poor comparative education. Unfortunately, to date, far too much of what passes for comparative education would fail on these essential tests.

Even in a single-country case study, it must be emphasized, only the most preliminary work can afford to proceed innocent of an explicitly stated hypothesis, clearly defined concepts and variables, and announcement of the minimum standards of proof to be accepted as validation of the hypothesis. Case studies that neglect these basic features of scientific work risk remaining isolated fragments of knowledge, unconnected to a wider understanding of the phenomena with which they deal. A series of separate country-by-country studies is no substitute for work that is overtly comparative from the beginning and is designed specifically to test hypotheses cross-nationally.

Although explanation is the ultimate aim of all scientific (and hence of all comparative) work in education, the process of explanation often yields some significant by-products. Important new information may be garnered about the educational and social systems of the world; concepts that previously appeared to have universal validity may be tested against the variety of global experience and shown to have validity only under certain specified conditions; and help may be provided to planners trying to improve the effectiveness of educational systems. None of these by-products of the scientific, comparative enterprise is to be despised. Indeed, frustrated by the complexities of the problems we choose to examine and the inadequacy of the tools at our command, they may turn out to be the only secure fruits of our labors, and we may need to console ourselves with the thought that half a loaf is better than none. But insofar as investigators actually prefer the by-products of quanta of information or concept-validation to the main goal of explanation, they are settling for second-best. Without doubt, there is a place for work that sets out simply to collect cross-national material, describe phenomena, and classify data. For example, in the literature of comparative education there are many studies of curricular developments, examination requirements, enrollment patterns, administrative structures, modes of financial provision, and so forth. Furthermore, the continual updating and extension of such compendia and catalogs is a necessary and valuable contribution. But devising and developing a taxonomy of comparative education items is only a preliminary of, and perhaps a concomitant to fruitful comparative work. In no sense does it penetrate to the core of the undertaking. The scholar who collects data on, say, teacher-training practices for European secondary education, arranges them in convenient categories, discusses the validity of the categories and the reliability of the information, and goes no further, is stopping short just at the point where a comparative *investigation* begins. He can, and often does, suggest tentative explanations for some of the phenomena he has uncovered, but it is the precise formulation of hypotheses, discussion of the theoretical justifications for advancing them, and the statement and operationalizing of concepts and indicators that represents the essence of comparative work in education. It goes far beyond the business of assembling data simply for informational purposes, important and difficult though even that task may be.

A special question arises concerning the role of history in comparative education. The historian aims at providing what is called genetic explanation of events in time; that is, he endeavors to demonstrate how particular events were caused by a convergence of prior happenings, forces, and factors. Thus, the historian attempts to explain the Education Act of 1944 in Britain by referring to the variety of social, political, and education phenomena preceding the passage of the bill into law. Comparative educators, using historical approaches, have attempted to make genetic explanations of educational phenomena on a cross-national basis, and in the process have written some extraordinarily insightful and readable books. But these studies share the weakness of most traditional historical studies: their conclusions rely largely on the private insights of their authors, not only regarding which categories are valid and which data are relevant, but also on the matter of what quantity and quality of evidence constitute proof of a particular assertion. The new history recognizes these difficulties in the older style of historical work and is moving towards a more empirical and, where possible, quantified approach. As this movement succeeds in establishing in historical studies what is essentially the approach advocated throughout this volume, empirically-oriented comparative educators will acquire an additional instrument for their work. To the scholarly insights of the old historians will be added a measure of the empirical rigor of the new, to the benefit of both.

The criteria of the empirically based social sciences are not offered as a simple nostrum for all the unsolved problems of comparative education. Indeed, advocacy of the scientific approach adds a host of new difficulties to the many already evident. The problems involved in proceeding toward rigorous, scientific explanation in comparative education are not to be dismissed lightly. In education, as in the wider social context, both data and concepts are far from satisfactory. Data abound in some areas while remaining quite scanty elsewhere. Not only is the accuracy of much of the available statistical information highly questionable, but the reliability of nonquantified, descriptive material is very limited. More confusing still, the margin of error or the extent of unreliability is unpredictable, varying according to the country observed, the date of collection, and the kinds of data reported. Concepts tend to be at least as elusive. For example, the common use of such terms as democracy, socialization, or even secondary education as categories for observing, grouping and interpreting data cannot be satisfactory in the absence of agreement on operational definitions. Yet even generally acceptable, functional definitions are difficult to achieve. Perhaps comparative education is suffering more from the imprecisions inherent in the term education than from vagueness in the term comparative, but whatever the source of the difficulty, typologies and explanatory concepts in comparative education remain crude, questionable, and largely unvalidated. Data and concepts tend to be narrowly ad hoc, and notions of causality are at best primitive. These are the hallmarks of any field of study in the first stages of its search for a distinguishing methodology and universe of discourse.

Concern with data and definition of concepts must not be allowed to obscure a more important goal, that of exploiting the full explanatory and instrumental values of comparative studies in education. Though the explanatory value of work motivated by the desire to import foreign educational practices or to develop a spirit of international harmony has not been high, there is a sense in which useful lessons can be learned from abroad. Sir Michael Sadler was right when he saw the practical value of studying foreign education and society in the chance to improve the understanding of one's own country. Isaac Kandel, too, was right when he viewed each nation's educational system as a species of laboratory where a particular attempt was being made to solve a more general set of social, political and historical problems. But realization of the instrumental and learning potential of comparative education depends upon using a method that will avoid the a priori judgments and biases that have characterized so much of the earlier work. As one observer has put it, the instrumental value of comparative study is great, provided one can avoid the three main traps of foreign observation: the Pago-Pago fallacy, which tends to say of everything, "How quaint!"; the Victorian lady-in-waiting fallacy, which leads us to wrinkle our noses in disgust and exclaim, "How wrong!"; and the Judy O'Grady fallacy, which dismisses the wild variety of human experience with the easy plea, "It's the same the whole world over!"[1] Especially in studying foreign nations and cultures, bias is a major problem, whether it stems from a conscious attempt of the investigator to prove a case for the superiority or inferiority of his own country's education, or from an unconscious imposition on data and conclusions of merely personal or parochial values implicitly assumed to be universal.

Although there are grave problems inherent in every effort to study education and society comparatively, and severe additional problems raised by attempts to apply social science techniques to comparative work, the promise both of the general field of comparative education and of the specific methods advocated here remains great. The potential of the field, as we have argued, lies first in the promise of extending the generality of propositions beyond the confines of a single society; second, in the provision of an arena where propositions, testable only in a cross-national context, can be investigated; third, as a field for interdisciplinary work; and finally, as an instrument for planners and policy makers.

These potentialities will be realized only if satisfactory criteria for assessing contributions to comparative education can be developed. This in turn is contingent upon securing convincing methods of validating research findings. Intuitive studies, even when bent on explanation and concerned with causation, provide inadequate proof; empirical investigation offers the hope of a more satisfactory system of validation. It provides an instrument for cutting through the circularities of reasoning inherent in even the best of the tradi-

---

[1] V. R. Lorwin, *The French Labour Movement.* Cambridge, Mass.: Harvard University Press, 1955, p. xvii.

tional studies. On the other hand, a purely inductive approach cannot be advocated. Simply to roam over the facts and to draw generalizations from them invites repetition of the errors of the past: encyclopedism (only now perhaps rendered more economical by the efficiency of electronic computers), observer bias and arbitrariness, and absence of criteria to guide the observer on the questions of which data are important and how many are enough.

A method that incorporates the intuitive insights and speculative reflections of the observer, but submits them to systematic, empirical testing appears to offer the best hope for the progress of comparative education. It provides teachers with something teachable and students with something eminently learnable and useful. Furthermore, it provides a criterion for evaluating research in comparative education, since each step in the process of investigation is always open to scrutiny, and conclusions and inferences are publicly arrived at. Researchers find built in to the hypothetico-inductive approach the expectation that their inquiries will be replicated and the validity of their data, methods, and conclusions subjected to the critical inspection of peers. Finally, because it is heuristic and open-ended, the social scientific method offers the researchers of one generation the hope of building securely on the work of their predecessors.

Clearer aims when doing research and more precise criteria after research has been completed are the essential requirements at the present stage of comparative study. The comparative educator needs to start with the questions: "Where do I want to go?" and "How will I know when I have arrived?" for the answers point the way toward an influential, intellectually cogent, and elegant science of comparative education.

APPENDIXES

Appendix A

Further Data and Manipulations on Two Model Hypotheses

Model Hypothesis 1

1. DATA ON EDUCATIONAL AND ECONOMIC LEVEL FOR ALL COUNTRIES

Table 9 presents the raw data for each indicator used in the first model hypothesis, for the seventy-two countries for which information was available. The tables in Part Three of the text (Tables 1, 2, 6, and 7) are based on this information, and use rankings within the selected samples for comparison.

GNP per capita is expressed in United States dollar equivalents for the year 1955 or the nearest year available.
Growth rate is the average annual rate of growth of GNP (1957/ 1958–1964/1965), expressed as a percentage.

Table 9. Data on All Countries: Educational and Economic Indicators

	GNP Per Capita	Educational Indicators			Economic Growth Rate
		Enrollment	Expenditure	Illiteracy	
	Y	S	E	L	G
Afghanistan	54	4	—	—	10.2
Argentina	374	72	3.2	10.5*	0.3
Australia	1215	90	3.0	—	2.4
Austria	532	72	4.0	—	3.9
Belgium	1015	91	2.3	—	3.4
Bolivia	66	35	—	67.9	1.4
Brazil	262	37	2.2	44.9*	1.3
Bulgaria	285	72	2.8	14.7	11.4
Burma	52	33	2.5	42.3	2.2
Canada	1667	79	3.9	—	5.2
Ceylon	122	65	3.1	32.2	0.2
Chile	180	69	1.8	18.6*	1.1
China, Rep. of	102	69	1.8	46.1	4.5
Colombia	330	41	1.4	37.7	1.9
Costa Rica	307	70	—	18.7*	0.3
Cyprus	374	73	3.6	29.6*	3.9
Czechoslovakia	543	79	—	—	3.7
Denmark	913	90	3.8	—	4.8
Dominican Rep.	205	61	—	40.1	0.8
Ecuador	204	47	1.5*	39.5*	1.5
Egypt	133	36	3.8	80.5	10.4
El Salvador	244	40	—	55.7*	2.5
Ethiopia	54	3	—	—	2.7
Finland	941	83	4.9*	—	10.1
France	1046	87	2.4	—	3.7
Germany, Fed. Rep.	762	87	3.5	—	4.3
Ghana	135	28	2.5	—	2.8
Greece	239	70	1.3	23.4*	6.3
Guatemala	179	27	1.5	70.6	2.3
Haiti	75	23	1.1	89.5	2.1
Honduras	137	33	1.1	61.5*	0.9
Hungary	387	74	5.0	3.8*	7.1
India	72	25	2.0	77.3*	1.8
Iran	100	19	—	87.2	2.1
Iraq	195	26	2.8	85.5	4.4
Ireland	509	99	3.4	—	3.9

Table 9. Data on All Countries: Educational and Economic Indicators (continued)

| | GNP Per Capita | Educational Indicators | | | Economic Growth Rate |
		Enrollment	Expenditure	Illiteracy	
	Y	S	E	L	G
Israel	540	89	—	9.4*	7.4
Italy	442	57	2.7	11.8*	5.1
Japan	240	92	6.1	2.2	10.2
Jordan	96	54	—	—	6.2
Korea	80	60	—	23.2	3.2
Malaysia	298	47	—	52.5	2.7
Mexico	187	47	0.9	38.8	2.7
Morocco	159	17	—	86.2	0.0
Netherlands	708	92	2.9	—	3.6
New Zealand	1249	92	3.5	—	2.5
Nicaragua	254	37	—	57.3	2.6
Nigeria	70	22	—	88.5	2.6
Norway	969	87	4.1	—	3.9
Pakistan	56	23	0.5	81.1	2.5
Panama	350	62	3.9	30.1	4.7
Paraguay	108	60	1.3	30.7	0.8
Peru	140	46	2.1	39.4	3.9
Philippines	201	70	2.4	33.1*	1.2
Poland	468	68	—	5.4*	4.4
Portugal	201	54	1.8	41.1*	6.3
Puerto Rico	511	90	6.6	23.0	12.0
Rumania	320	50	—	11.4	10.3
S. Africa, Rep.	381	56	4.0	69.9*	3.0
Spain	254	59	1.3*	15.5*	6.1
Sudan	100	6	—	88.0	1.5
Sweden	1165	83	2.6	—	4.2
Switzerland	1229	69	2.7	—	3.1
Thailand	100	46	—	38.3	4.4
Tunisia	131	27	—	84.3	2.3
Turkey	276	36	1.5	65.0	1.5
U. S. S. R.	682	80*	5.5*	1.5	6.1
United Kingdom	998	82	4.3	—	2.8
U. S. A.	2343	102	4.0	2.7*	2.4
Venezuela	762	47	2.1	41.6*	1.5
Yugoslavia	297	58	2.0*	27.3	9.0

Sources: Data adapted from Norton Ginsburg, *Atlas of Economic Development* (Chicago: University of Chicago Press, 1961), p. 18; UNESCO *Statistical Yearbook 1965* (Paris: UNESCO, 1966), pp. 36–46, 117–137, 342–364.
* Estimates from data for nearest year available. Blanks indicate data not available.

Educational measures are percentages of the year 1955, or the nearest year available:

Enrollment measures the percentage of school age population enrolled in school (primary and secondary).

Expenditure represents the percentage of the national budget spent on education.

Illiteracy is the percentage of illiterates in the total population.

2. SUMMARY OF FINDINGS WITH RANDOM SAMPLE

In Part Three two "judgment" groups of countries (high-growth and low-growth) were used to test the hypothesis. Alternatively, a random sample may be selected. Every fifth country from the alphabetized list of seventy-two countries in Table 9 was taken, ranked on each indicator within the sample, and subjected to the same procedures as in Part Three. The results for these fourteen countries are presented in Table 10.

Testing with a random sample tends to confirm the hypothesis. Countries with educational level higher than economic level ($D > 0$) generally have higher subsequent growth rates than countries with low relative educational level ($D < 0$). Weighting the growth rates of each country by its D-value strengthens the confirmation of the hypothesis.

3. SUMMARY OF FINDINGS WITH SAMPLE OF COUNTRIES, SELECTED ACCORDING TO ECONOMIC LEVEL

The economic and social structures of rich and poor countries differ greatly, irrespective of their economic growth rates. Presumably then, a useful basis for sampling is to select countries according to levels of wealth rather than growth rates. Selecting a sample of countries at similar levels of wealth would then serve as a rough means of holding constant, and thus controlling for the effect of the important variable, economic level.

Table 10. Random Sample: A Comparison of Educational-Economic Profile and Subsequent Economic Growth (based on rankings)

	Educational Indicators							Growth Rates by Groups			
								Unweighted		Weighted	
	GNP per Capita	Enroll-ment	Expendi-ture	Illiter-acy	Composite Education Index	Educational-Economic Profile	Economic Growth Rate				
	Y	s	E	L	C	D	G	D > 0	D < 0	D > 0	D < 0
Belgium	3	2	7.0		4.5	−1.5	3.4		3.4		5.1
Canada	1	4	1.4		2.7	−1.7	5.2		5.2		8.8
Costa Rica	7	5		3.1	4.1	2.9	0.3	0.3		0.9	
Ecuador	9	8½	10.5	4.7	7.9	1.1	1.5	1.5		1.7	
France	2	3	5.6		4.3	−2.3	3.7		3.7		8.5
Haiti	13	12½	12.6	14.0	13.1	−.1	2.1		2.1		0.2
Iraq	10	11	4.2	10.8	8.7	1.3	4.4	4.4		5.7	
Jordan	12	7			7.0	5.0	6.2	6.2		31.0	
Netherlands	5	1	2.8		1.9	3.1	3.6	3.6		11.2	
Pakistan	14	12½	14.0	9.3	11.9	2.1	2.5	2.5		5.2	
Poland	6	6		1.6	3.8	2.2	4.4	4.4		9.7	
Sudan	11	14		12.4	13.2	−2.2	1.5		1.5		3.3
Turkey	8	10	10.5	7.8	9.4	−1.4	1.5		1.5		2.1
Venezuela	4	8½	8.4	6.2	7.7	−3.7	1.5		1.5		5.6
							ΣG = 22.9	22.9	18.9	65.4	33.6
							N = 7	7	7	17.7	12.9
							Ḡ = 3.3	3.3	2.7	3.7	2.6

Sources: Data adapted from Norton Ginsburg, *Atlas of Economic Development* (Chicago: University of Chicago Press, 1961), p. 18; UNESCO *Statistical Yearbook 1965* (Paris: UNESCO, 1966), pp. 36–46, 117–137, 342–364.

(a) The results of investigating hypothesis 1 with a sample of twenty-four wealthy countries (GNP per capita U.S. $440 and above), using the same procedures as in Part Three, are presented in Table 11. Briefly, the hypothesis is confirmed very strongly for both unweighted and weighted figures. Furthermore, the greater the disparity between educational and economic levels (that is, the higher the absolute value of D, irrespective of whether it is positive or negative), the greater the rate of subsequent economic growth (see Figure, p. 202).

(b) Complementing the previous test with a sample of wealthy countries, another group of twenty-four poor countries (GNP per capita below U.S. $181) was investigated using the same procedures. One result tends to refute the hypothesis: countries in this sample with low relative educational levels tend to have slightly higher growth rates than those with high relative educational levels. However, in the countries where educational level was considerably higher than economic level, subsequent growth rates were higher than in countries with extremely low relative educational levels. Consequently, the results can only be called ambiguous.

Final figures of average growth rates were as follows:

$D > 0$	$D < 0$	
2.7	3.2	(unweighted)
3.0	1.9	(weighted)

4. SUMMARY OF FINDINGS FROM TOTAL SAMPLE (SEVENTY-TWO COUNTRIES)

The final sample subjected to the same set of procedures was the total group of seventy-two countries in Table 9. In general, the hypothesis was confirmed. Countries with high relative educational level (positive D) tended to have higher subsequent growth rates than countries with negative D.

Moreover, countries with very high positive D-values tended to have higher subsequent growth rates than countries with very low negative D-values. However, as a general rule, countries with very

Table 11. **High Economic Level: A Comparison of Educational-Economic Profile and Subsequent Economic Growth** (based on rankings)

	GNP Per Capita	Educational Indicators				Educational-Economic Profile	Economic Growth Rate	Growth Rates by Groups			
		Enroll-ment	Expendi-ture	Illiteracy	Composite Ed. Index			Unweighted		Weighted	
	Y	s	E	L	C	D	G	D > 0	D < 0	D > 0	D < 0
U.S.A.	1	1	7.4	6	4.8	-3.8	2.4	n.a.*	2.4	n.a.	9.2
Canada	2	17½	9.6	—	13.6	-11.6	5.2	n.a.	5.2	n.a.	60.1
New Zealand	3	3½	12.6	—	8.2	-5.2	2.5	n.a.	2.5	n.a.	13.0
Switzerland	4	20	18.6	—	19.3	-15.3	3.1	n.a.	3.1	n.a.	47.4
Australia	5	7	15.6	—	11.3	-6.5	2.4	n.a.	2.4	n.a.	15.1
Sweden	6	13½	20.4	—	17.0	-11.0	4.2	n.a.	4.2	n.a.	46.0
France	7	11	21.6	—	16.3	-9.3	3.7	n.a.	3.7	n.a.	34.4
Belgium	8	5	22.8	—	13.9	-5.9	3.4	n.a.	3.4	n.a.	20.2
United Kingdom	9	15	4.8	—	9.9	-0.9	2.8	n.a.	2.8	n.a.	2.5
Norway	10	11	6.0	—	8.5	1.5	3.9	3.9	n.a.	5.8	n.a.
Finland	11	13½	3.6	—	8.6	2.4	10.1	10.1	n.a.	24.7	n.a.
Denmark	12	7	10.8	—	8.9	3.1	4.8	4.8	n.a.	14.9	n.a.
Germany	13½	11	12.6	—	11.8	1.7	4.3	4.3	n.a.	7.3	n.a.
Venezuela	13½	24	24.0	24	24.0	-10.5	1.5	n.a.	1.5	n.a.	15.8
Netherlands	15	16	16.8	3	10.2	4.8	3.6	3.6	n.a.	17.5	n.a.
U.S.S.R.	16	22	2.4	15	7.1	8.9	6.0	6.0	n.a.	53.6	n.a.
Uruguay	17	17½	—	—	18.5	-1.5	-1.3	n.a.	-1.3	n.a.	-2.0
Czechoslovakia	18	17½	—	12	17.5	0.5	3.7	3.7	n.a.	1.9	n.a.
Israel	19	9	7.8	—	10.5	8.5	7.4	7.4	n.a.	62.9	n.a.
Australia	20	19	1.2	—	13.4	6.6	3.9	3.9	n.a.	25.7	n.a.
Puerto Rico	21	7	—	21	9.7	11.3	12.0	12.0	n.a.	135.2	n.a.
Ireland	22	2	14.4	—	8.2	13.8	3.9	3.9	n.a.	53.8	n.a.
Poland	23	21	—	9	15.0	8.0	4.4	4.4	n.a.	35.2	n.a.
Italy	24	23	18.6	18	19.9	4.1	5.1	5.1	n.a.	21.1	n.a.

$\Sigma G = 73.2$ $N = 13$ $\bar{G} = 5.6$ | Unweighted $D < 0$: 29.9 / 11 / 2.7 | Weighted $D > 0$: 459.7 / 75.3 / 6.1 | Weighted $D < 0$: 261.6 / 81.1 / 3.2

Sources: Data adapted from Norton Ginsburg, *Atlas of Economic Development* (Chicago: University of Chicago Press, 1961), p. 18; UNESCO *Statistical Yearbook 1965* (Paris: UNESCO, 1966), pp. 36–46, 117–137, 342–364.
* n.a. = not applicable.

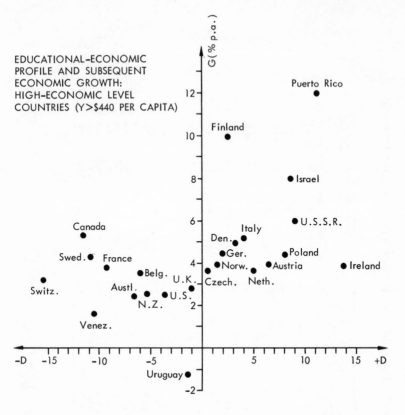

EDUCATIONAL-ECONOMIC
PROFILE AND SUBSEQUENT
ECONOMIC GROWTH:
HIGH-ECONOMIC LEVEL
COUNTRIES (Y>$440 PER CAPITA)

high *or* very low relative educational levels tended to have subsequent growth rates noticeably lower, on average, than countries with educational level fairly close to economic level.

We may infer from these results that, whereas a positive educational-economic profile is associated with greater economic growth, countries perform better in terms of subsequent growth if their educational levels do not get too far out of line with their economic levels. This conclusion might in turn be subjected to empirical testing.

Final figures of average growth rates for this large sample of seventy-two countries were as follows:

D > 0	D < 0	
4.3	3.0	(unweighted)
4.2	2.8	(weighted)

Model Hypothesis 2

5. EXAMPLES OF QUANTIFYING THE CONCEPT OTHERWORLDLINESS

> *Whatever exists at all exists in some amount. To know it thoroughly involves knowing its quantity as well as its quality.*   E. L. THORNDIKE

Intuition suggests that some religions are more otherworldly than other, but precision requires careful analysis of the constituent elements of the concept (see discussion in Chapter 13), evaluation of the significance of particular items of information, and comparisons among religions on each of the selected elements before a total comparison can be made. In model hypothesis 2, five major indicators were identified to span the several dimensions of the concept of otherworldliness (see Chapter 15). Each religion was assigned a number for each indicator and the numerical values were added to arrive at an otherworldliness score for each. Table 3 summarized the conclusions of this process, in which a simple ranking procedure was used within each of the two samples (of four and five religions respectively) considered separately. Thus, for the first indicator or element in otherworldliness (H = importance of the hereafter), in the sample Catholic, Hindu, Islamic and Buddhist countries, it was necessary to review the literature to judge how central to each religion was the belief in the hereafter, which was present in varying amounts in all of them. The conclusion was that the hereafter was least important in Buddhism and most important in Hinduism. Consequently, in the group of four ideologies, Buddhism was assigned the number 1, and Hinduism, 4.

Religions were ranked similarly on the second indicator, priesthood (P). In Hinduism, the existence of a learned caste, which includes the priesthood and which is extremely exclusive by definition, suggests that Hinduism should receive the highest score on this indicator. On the other hand, in Islam there is no priestly class or caste and, though holy men exist, they are not necessary for an individual's performance of his religious duties. In both Catholicism and Buddhism, the priesthood is not drawn from a special caste or class as in Hinduism, but it is sharply differentiated from the lay population by training, priestly vows, and way of life. In Catholicism, however, unlike Buddhism, the priest acts as the indispensable intermediary between man and the deity. From this brief summary of judgments, the priesthood was differentiated among the religions as follows, in rank order from least to most important: Islamic (1), Buddhist (2), Catholic (3), Hindu (4).

Another example of the same process is drawn from the sample of five Christian denominations. For the eschatological dimension of otherworldliness, Catholicism appeared to place the hereafter in a more fundamental or central position in the total religious ideology than any of the others in the sample. Lutheranism, with its heavy emphasis on Hell, was assigned to the next position, followed by Presbyterianism. Anglicanism, it was considered, stressed the importance of retribution or reward in afterlife less than any of the named Christian religions, but all gave it more attention than Judaism. In this way numbers were assigned from 5 (Catholicism) to 1 (Judaism).

After achieving otherworldliness scores for each religion, it was necessary to adjust them in accordance with variations from country to country in the degree and forms of influence of a given religion. For this, see the discussion on religiosity and manipulations leading to an adjusted index of otherworldliness in Chapter 15 and Table 4.

Appendix B
Some Sample Hypotheses for Testing

The following list of hypotheses was originally devised to suggest subjects for investigation by students in an introductory course in Comparative Education at the graduate level.[1] The hypotheses are offered for illustrative purposes only and in order to encourage two types of exercises.

First, students can use this list as preliminary material from which to design hypotheses more closely suited to their own particular interests, backgrounds, and skills. Some of the hypotheses are better than others: they are more specific, important, explanatory, manageable, and heuristic. Others may strike the reader as vague, trivial, descriptive, untestable, or devoid of further implications for testing. In no sense should this list be regarded as an assortment of instant hypotheses, ready to be worked without further development and refinement.

Second, the list will suggest some topics for structured investigations using cross-national data, in which students systematically go

[1] Noah, Harold J., and M. A. Eckstein. "A Design for Teaching 'Comparative Education,'" *Comparative Education Review*, 10 (1966), 511–513.

through the major steps of a scientific study of a problem, identifying the possibilities and limitations at each stage: operationalizing the concepts, selecting the countries, collecting data and manipulating them, and drawing inferences.

It will be noted that each hypothesis postulates a relationship between some dimension of education and some dimension of the social structure or the economy, or the religious, political or social ideology, all of which are parts of the total environment within which educational phenomena exist and with which they interact.

1. The more authoritarian the political system:
   a. the earlier specialization begins in school curricula;
   b. the less comprehensive the secondary schools;
   c. the more centralized the administration of education;
   d. the more male-dominated the educational system.
2. The more democratic the polity:
   a. the more child-centered the teaching;
   b. the more nonrepresentational the art work of school-children;
   c. the greater the professional autonomy of teachers;
   d. the lower the social status of teachers.
3. The greater the concern for political orthodoxy, the more centralized the school system.
4. The greater a country's involvement in foreign wars, the greater the increase in its educational effort.
5. The more imperialistic the polity:
   a. the less recognition of adolescence as a discrete developmental stage;
   b. the more punitive the school regime.
6. The less politically stable a country, the greater the rate of educational change.
7. Educational revolutions are consequences, not causes, of political revolutions.
8. The "newer" the nation, the greater the participation of ex-schoolteachers in government.
9. School systems in communist countries are designed to serve the interests of the state more than are schools in noncommunist countries.

10. School systems in noncommunist countries are designed to serve the needs of individual students more than are schools in communist countries.

11. Among Christian countries, the more Catholic the country, the lower its educational level.

12. The more Protestant a country, the more extensive the provision for public education.

13. The larger the fraction of the population belonging to a single religious denomination, the less tolerance of religious nonconformity within the schools.

14. Among Christian countries, the more Protestant the country, the more numerous the schools of religious nonconformity.

15. The greater the degree of religious heterogeneity of the population:
    a. the more secular the public schools;
    b. the clearer the distinction between private and public schools.

16. The more otherworldly the religious beliefs, the less developed the educational system.

17. The more restricted the opportunities for secondary and/or higher education:
    a. the lower the amount of social mobility;
    b. the greater the distance among social classes;
    c. the more aristocratic the social and political elites.

18. The larger the middle class in the stratification system:
    a. the longer the period of common schooling;
    b. the greater the emphasis on humanistic studies;
    c. the less punitive the school regime.

19. The more varied the social class composition of the student body in higher education (and/or secondary education), the greater the amount of student unrest.

20. The longer the average length of schooling of the population, the fewer the external marks of class difference.

21. The less marked the physical differences associated with race, the greater the equality of educational provision among races.

22. There is no relationship between the degree of racial homogeneity in the population at large, and/or the school population, and:

    a.   standards of educational attainment;
    b.   turnover rates of teachers;
    c.   student indiscipline;
    d.   expenditures per pupil.
23. The more developed the economy:
    a.   the more democratic the educational system;
    b.   the greater the emphasis on technical studies in the curricula.
24. The larger the fraction of GNP devoted to education:
    a.   the more centralized the education system;
    b.   the more national planning of education;
    c.   the higher the quality of education.
25. The greater the equality of educational provision, the narrower the range of income differentials in the community.
26. The greater the investment in primary/ secondary/ higher/ technical/ liberal arts education, the more advanced the level of economic development.
27. The smaller the ratio between enrollments in higher education and enrollments in primary education, the lower the rate of growth of GNP.
28. The lower the pupil/teacher ratio, the higher the rate of growth of the GNP.
29. There can be no modernization of education without urbanization.
30. Educational innovation is extensive in wealthy and poor countries; it is more limited in countries at middle economic levels.

ENVOI

There are many aphorisms and proverbs that refer to education, heredity, upbringing of children, and so on. Often they contain in compressed form the material for a hypothesis—a hypothesis that, moreover, might even be testable.

The reader is invited to try his hand at casting one or more of the following aphorisms into a form suitable for cross-national testing:

1. Le style, c'est l'homme.
2. Spare the rod, and spoil the child.
3. The Battle of Waterloo was won on the playing fields of Eton.
4. Penny wise, pound foolish.
5. Open a school, and close a prison.
6. Der Apfel fällt nicht weit vom Baum.
7. Nobody ever died of a split infinitive.
8. The pen is mightier than the sword.
9. History is bunk.
10. The hand that rocks the cradle rules the world.
11. ЯЗЫК--МАТЬ НАРОДА
12. 黄金滿籯不如遺子一經

Selected Bibliography

Theory and Methodology in the Social Sciences

Bell, Daniel. "Twelve Modes of Prediction," *Penguin Survey of the Social Sciences,* ed. Julius Gould. Harmondsworth, Middlesex: Penguin Books, 1965, pp. 96–127.

Direnzo, Gordon J. (ed.). *Concepts, Theory, and Explanation in the Behavioral Sciences.* New York: Random House, 1966.

Duverger, Maurice. *Introduction to the Social Sciences,* trans. Malcolm Anderson. London: Allen and Unwin, 1964.

Fleron, Frederic J., Jr. "Soviet Area Studies and the Social Sciences: Some Methodological Problems in Communist Studies," *Soviet Studies,* **XIX** (June 1968), 313–339.

Hempel, Carl G. "Explanation and Laws," *Theories of History,* ed. Patrick Gardiner. New York: The Free Press, 1959, pp. 344–356.

———— and Paul Oppenheim. "The Logic of Explanation," *Readings in the Philosophy of Science,* eds. Herbert Feigel and May Brodbeck. New York: Appleton-Century-Crofts, 1953, pp. 319–352.

Kerlinger, Fred N. *Foundations of Behavioral Research*. New York: Holt, Rinehart and Winston, 1965.

Madge, John. *The Tools of Social Science*. New York: Doubleday and Company, Anchor Books, 1965.

Merritt, Richard L., and Stein Rokkan (eds.). *Comparing Nations: The Use of Quantitative Data in Cross-National Research*. New Haven: Yale University Press, 1966.

Nagel, Ernest. *The Structure of Science: Problems in the Logic of Scientific Explanation*. New York: Harcourt, Brace and World, 1961, chaps. 13 and 14.

Popper, Karl R. *The Logic of Scientific Discovery*. New York: Harper and Row, Harper Torchbooks, 1965.

Sjoberg, Gideon. "The Comparative Method in the Social Sciences," *Philosophy of Science*. 22 (April 1955), 106–117.

Toulmin, Stephen. *The Philosophy of Science: An Introduction*. New York: Harper and Row, 1960.

Theory and Methodology in Comparative Education

Anderson, C. Arnold. "Methodology of Comparative Education," *International Review of Education*, 7 (1961), 1–23.

Bereday, George Z. F. *Comparative Method in Education*. New York: Holt, Rinehart, and Winston, 1964.

—— "Reflections on Comparative Methodology in Education, 1964–1966," *Comparative Education*, 3 (1967), 169–187.

Edding, Friedrich. "The Use of Economics in Comparing Educational Systems," *International Review of Education*, XI (1965), 453–465.

Foshay, Arthur. "The Uses of Empirical Methods in Comparative Education: a Pilot Study to Extend the Scope," *International Review of Education*, 9 (1963–1964), 257–268.

Foster, Philip. "Comparative Methodology and the Study of African Education," *Comparative Education Review*, 4 (October 1960), 110–117.

Holmes, Brian. "The Problem Approach in Comparative Education: Some Methodological Considerations," *Comparative Education Review*, 2 (June 1958), 3–8.

Kandel, I. L. "The Methodology of Comparative Education," *International Review of Education*, V (1959), 270–278.

Kazamias, Andreas M. "Some Old and New Approaches to Methodology in Comparative Education," *Comparative Education Review*, 5 (October 1961), 90–96.

King, Edmund. "Comparative Studies and Policy Decisions," *Comparative Education*, 4 (1967) 51–63.

Social Science Research

Adelman, Irma, Morris Adelman, and Cynthia Taft. *Society, Politics, and Economic Development: A Quantitative Approach*. Baltimore: The Johns Hopkins Press, 1967.

Almond, Gabriel A. and Sidney Verba. *The Civic Culture: Political Attitudes and Democracy in Five Nations*. Princeton: Princeton University Press, 1963.

—— and Coleman, James S. (ed.). *The Politics of the Developing Areas*. Princeton: Princeton University Press, 1960.

Apter, David E. *The Politics of Modernization*. Chicago: University of Chicago Press, 1965.

Black, C. E. *The Dynamics of Modernization: A Study in Comparative History*. New York: Harper and Row, Harper Torchbooks, 1967.

Bronfenbrenner, Urie. "Soviet Methods of Character Education: Some Implications for Research," *American Psychologist*, XVII (August 1962), 550–564.

Dahrendorf, Ralf. *Class and Class Conflict in Industrial Society*. Stanford, California: Stanford University Press, 1959.

Denison, Edward F. *Why Growth Rates Differ: Postwar Experience in Nine Western Countries*. Washington, D.C.: The Brookings Institution, 1967.

Eisenstadt, S. N. *Essays on Comparative Institutions*. New York: John Wiley and Sons, 1965.

Etzioni, Amitai. *A Comparative Analysis of Complex Organizations: on Power, Involvement and their Correlates.* New York: The Free Press, 1961.

Geertz, Clifford. *Peddlers and Princes; Social Change and Economic Modernization in Two Indonesian Towns.* Chicago: The University of Chicago Press, 1963.

Inkeles, Alex, and Peter Rossi. "National Comparisons of Occupational Prestige," *American Journal of Sociology,* **61** (1956), 1–31.

Lerner, Daniel. *The Passing of Traditional Society: Modernizing the Middle East.* New York: The Free Press, 1958.

Lipset, Seymour Martin. *The First New Nation: the United States in Historical and Comparative Perspective.* New York: Basic Books, 1963.

——— and Reinhard Bendix. *Social Mobility in Industrial Society.* Berkeley: University of California Press, 1963.

Marczewski, Jean. *Introduction à l'Histoire Quantitative.* Genève: Librairie Droz. 1965.

McClelland, David C. *The Achieving Society.* Princeton: D. Van Nostrand Company, 1961.

——— "Motivational Patterns in Southeast Asia with Special Reference to the Chinese Case," *The Journal of Social Issues,* **XIX** (January 1963), 6–19.

Miller, S. M. "Comparative Social Mobility," *Current Sociology,* **9** (1960), 1–88.

Richardson, Lewis F. *Statistics of Deadly Quarrels.* Chicago: Quadrangle Books, 1960.

Singer, J. David (ed.). *Quantitative International Politics: Insights and Evidence.* New York: The Free Press, 1968.

Comparative Education Research

Adams, Don, and Joseph P. Farrell (eds.). *Education and Social Development.* Syracuse, New York: Center for Development Education, Syracuse University, 1967.

Anderson, C. Arnold. "A Skeptical Note on the Relation of Vertical Mobility to Education," *American Journal of Sociology,* 66 (May 1961), 560–570.

———— and Mary Jean Bowman (eds.). *Education and Economic Development.* Chicago: Aldine Publishing Company, 1965.

Bennett, William S., Jr. "Educational Change and Economic Development," *Sociology of Education,* 40 (Spring 1967), 101–114.

Bowles, Frank H. *Access to Higher Education,* 4 vols. Paris: UNESCO, 1963–1965.

Curle, Adam. "Education, Politics, and Development," *Comparative Education Review,* 7 (February 1964), 226–245.

Feldmesser, Robert A. "Social Status and Access to Higher Education: A Comparison of the United States and the Soviet Union," *Harvard Educational Review,* 27 (Spring 1957), 92–106.

Harbison, Frederick, and Charles A. Myers. *Education, Manpower, and Economic Growth: Strategies of Human Resource Development.* New York: McGraw-Hill, 1964.

Havighurst, Robert J. "Education, Social Mobility and Social Change in Four Societies. A Comparative Study," *International Review of Education,* 4 (1958), 167–182.

Husén Torsten (ed.). *International Study of Achievement in Mathematics: A Comparison of Twelve Countries,* 2 vols. New York: John Wiley and Sons, International Project for the Evaluation of Educational Achievement, 1967.

Peaslee, Alexander L. "Primary School Enrollments and Economic Growth," *Comparative Education Review,* 11 (February 1967), 57–67.

Reifman, Lucille (ed.). *Financing of Education for Economic Growth.* Paris: Organisation for Economic Cooperation and Development, 1966.

Robinson, E. A. G., and J. E. Vaizey (eds.). *The Economics of Education.* London: Macmillan, 1966.

Sanders, Donald P. "Patterns of Educational Change During Economic Growth." Ph.D. dissertation, Stanford University, 1962.

Sources of Quantified Social and Educational Data

Banks, Arthur S., and Robert B. Textor. *A Cross-Polity Survey.* Cambridge: M.I.T. Press, 1963.

Ginsburg, Norton S. *Atlas of Economic Development.* Chicago: University of Chicago Press, 1961.

Russett, Bruce M., et al. *World Handbook of Political and Social Indicators.* New Haven: Yale University Press, 1964.

United Nations. *Statistical Yearbook.* New York: United Nations. (Annual).

UNESCO. *Statistical Yearbook.* Paris: Unesco. (Annual).

UNESCO. *World Survey of Education,* 4 vols. Paris: Unesco, 1955–1966.

United States Bureau of the Census. *Statistical Abstract of the United States.* Washington, D.C. (Annual).

Index

Academic respectability, pecking order in, 117–8

Agency for International Development (AID), 152 n.

AHbar as-Sin Wa l-Hind, 10 n.

Alexander I, 16

Alford, Robert R., 76 n.

Allardt, Erik, 107 n., 145 n.

Almond, Gabriel A., 91, 109 n.

American Journal of Education, 25–6

Ammoun, Charles D., 37 n.

Anderson, C. Arnold, 68–9, 74, 130 n., 177

Andrews, Fannie Fern, 35

Antiquarianism, 128

Apter, David E., 95 n.

Arnold Matthew: life and work, 18; methodological sophistication, 30, 31, 40, 45; on value of comparative study, 41–2

Bache, A. D.: methodology, 26, 27–8, 30, 81; problems in educational borrowing, 24; purpose of his work, 23

Bacon, Francis, 60

Balogh, Thomas, 66 n.

Banks, Arthur S., 72 n. 144 n.

Barnard, Henry: views on educational borrowing, 20, 24; work and methodology, 25–6

Basham, A. L., 12 n.

Baster, Nancy, 71–2, 131 n.

Bates, E. S., 9 n.

Beeby, C. E., 70 n.

Bell, Daniel, 105 n.

Bell-Lancaster system, 19

Bendix, Reinhard, 76

Bennett, William S., Jr., 70 n.

Benton, William, 87 n.

Bereday, George Z. F.: on cultural bias, 115 n.; on development of comparative education, 3 n., 48, 62 n.; method and techniques, 62 n., 63–5

Berelson, Bernard, 114 n.

Big-game hunting, 128

"Black box," 96

Bonaparte, Napoleon, 16

Botero, 9 n.

Bouquet, A. C., 159 n.

Bowman, Mary Jean, 68–9, 130 n., 177

Brewer, Walter, 22 n.

Brickman, William W., 3 n., 9–10

British Commonwealth Educational Cooperation Program, 38

Bronowski, J., 111

Bryce Commission on Secondary Education, 45

Carr, E. H., 97

Case studies, 28, 48–9, 186; limits of, 187

Causal explanation: absence of in comparative study, 32; not yet attained, 73–4; distinguished from knowledge of process, 95–6; not posited in model hypotheses, 134; not provided by correlation, 68; rise

DUE